The Uffizi

all the gallery room by room

Mannelli

EDITRICE

Scorcio degli Uffizi da Piazza Signoria

Inhalt

Cortile degli Uffizi

Beschreibung des Bauwerks

Die Uffizien sind aus zwei vollkommen parallelen Blöcken zusammengesetzt, die sich vom Signoriaplatz bis ans Arnoufer (Lungarno Archibusieri) ziehen. Die zwei Flügel sind hier durch einen Gang verbunden, der sich über eine breite, harmonievolle, dreibögige Arkade hebt. In deren Mittelteil, zwischen den Skulpturen il Rigore und l'Equità (Strenge und Rechtlichkeit) des Vincenzo Danti, befindet sich eine schöne Statue von Giambologna, die Cosimo den Ersten der Medici darstellt. Der Sohn von Giovanni dalle Bande Nere ist diesem Denkmal würdig, da gerade er das große Bauwerk errichten wollte. Die Westseite der Uffizien, kürzer als die ihr gegenüberliegende Ostseite, ist durch die Tür der Bittschriften, (porta delle Suppliche), ein Werk Buontalentis, mit dem antiken Palazzo della Zecca, in dem die wertvollen Gulden und Münzen geprägt wurden, verbunden. Die beiden Blöcke des Bauwerks werden durch starke und schlanke tuskanische Säulen, unterbrochen von mächtigen, rechteckigen Pfeilern, gestützt. In diesen Pfeilern befinden sich geräumige Nischen, die Vasari als

Hohlräume entworfen hat, und in die im 19. Jahrhundert Statuen gestellt wurdelche berühmte Toskaner darstellen. In den Säulenhallen – wenn man von der Piazza della Signoria ausgeht auf der linken Seite des Palastes, wo sich der Eingang des Museums befindet – stehen die Statuen Lorenzo il Magnifico und Cosimo il Vecchio, Werke des Gaetano Grazzini und Luigi Magi; vom ersten Pfeiler aus finden wir folgende Statuen: Andrea Orcagna von Niccolò Bazzanti, Nicola Pisano von Pio Fedi, Giotto da Vespignano von Giovanni Duprè, Donatello von Girolamo Torrini und Leon Battista Alberti von Giovanni Lusini, Leonardo da Vinci von Luigi Pampaloni, Michelangelo Buonarroti von Luigi Santarelli, Dante Alighieri von Emilio Demi, Francesco Guicciardini von Luigi Cartei, Francesco Petrarca, von Andrea Leoni, Giovanni Boccaccio von Odoardo Fantacchiotti, Niccolò Machiavelli von Lorenzo Bartolini.

Nach diesem Teil der Uffizien, stehen wir der kürzesten Seite des vasarischen Bauwerks gegenüber. Sie vereinigt den soeben von uns zurückgelegten Ost- mit dem gegenüberliegenden Westflügel. Wenn man von der Innensei-

3

Emilio Demi: Dante   Luigi Pampaloni: Leonardo   Luigi Santarelli: Michelangelo

degli Uberti by Francesco Pazzi, Pier Capponi by Torello Bacci, Giovanni dalle Bande Nere by Temistocle Guerrazzi and Francesco Ferrucci by Pasquale Romanelli.

Let's turn now to the west wing. Close to the statue of Ferrucci we find the statue of Anteo Micheli (a botanist and geologist who lived between the 17th and 18th century) executed by Vincenzo Costani. Then we see in the following order Francesco Redi by Pietro Costa, Paolo Mascagni by Ludovico Caselli, Andrea Cesalpino by Pio Fedi, Sant'Antonino by Giovanni Duprè, Accursio by Odoardo Fantacchiotti, Guido d'Arezzo by Lorenzo Nencini and finally Benvenuto Cellini by Ulisse Cambi.

Above the beautiful arcade on the ground floor three different kinds of opening give the great building a more slender appearance. In fact, the architect wrote: «I have never built anything more difficult or more dangerous, for it is built on the river and almost in the air». Vasari was justified in his claims, since the facade of the Uffizi is a true piece of open-work. A row of wide windows, each one protected by a smalla, graceful balcony, is set on a series of square openings that alternate with classically-shaped pilaster strips. Above is the loggia which Vasari planned as an open gallery and which later was closed by Buontalenti with a series of large windows. The large U-shaped corridor from which one enters the rooms of the museum is covered with valuable frescoes. In fact, the corridor that runs along the east side of the building is decorated with grotesques, mythological scenes and landscapes painted by Alessandro Allori, Giovanni Butteri, Alessandro Puroni and Giovanni Bizzelli. The part that connects the east wing with the west wing was decorated about the middle of the 17th century by Cosimo Ulivelli, Angelo Gori, Jacopo Chiavistelli, Giuseppe Torrelli and Giuseppe Masini. These artists also painted the third part of the gallery, covering it with landscapes, portraits and allegorical scenes. Part of this work was destroyed in the fire of 1762; but some years later Giuseppe del Moro, Giuliano Traballesi and Giuseppe Terreni tried to reproduce the lost frescoes.

The church of San Pietro a Scheraggio

One of the buildings that Vasari demolished in order to erect the new Uffizi palace was the ancient church of San Pietro a Scheraggio. This church was built during the 11th century on the ruins of an even more ancient temple (9th century). It was consecrated in 1065 and immediately became one of the most important public buildings. It was a very large structure consisting of three aisles which were almost fifty metres long. The importance and the age of the church of San Pietro made it the source of some curious legends: for example, people said that the pulpit (now in the church of San Leonardo at Arcetri) and the marble rose-window of the facade were war booty. Rumour had it that these ornaments had been plundered from nearby Fiesole in 1125, when the old Etruscan village was conquered by its powerful rival Florence. On this subject Bartolomeo Rustichi wrote: « There was once the beautiful, ancient church of San Piero Ischeragio. It is said that in the year 1110 the Florentines took the city of Fiesole and destroyed it except for the Bishop's residence and certain churches: and then the Florentines obtained a marble eye that looks like a round wheel, took it from the church and set it in the eye of San Piero Ischeragio where it stands today». *This legend took root in Florence and even chroniclers as famous as Giovanni Villani held it to be true, adding that the rose-window was none other than the wheel of the marble* «carroccio» *of Fiesole. (A cart which accompanied the army and bore the standard of an Italian free city in the Middle Ages).*

So much folklore was due to the political importance of the church, for it was there that the Priors and Gonfaloniers of Justice took their oath of office and it was also the place where important political meetings were held. For a long time the walls of San Piero bore silent witness to the often dramatic events that took place in Florence. In 1267 they saw how the Guelfi family, furious in their thirst for revenge, violated the graves of the Uberti, traditionally buried in this church; they were present at the publication of the Ordinamenti di Giustizia *by Giano della Bella; they heard*

S. Piero a Scheraggio

Andrea del Castagno: F. Petrarca

das antike Monument an Wichtigkeit. 1410 wurde beschlossen das linke Schiff niederzureißen, um die Via della Ninna zu vergrößern. Als Vasari dann sein Meisterwerk errichtete, wurde die S. Piero-Kirche in die Uffizien eingegliedert, blieb jedoch bis 1743 ein heiliger Ort. In jenem Jahr beschloß man, das Hinterbliebene der antiken Kirche als Archiv zu verwenden.

Von S. Piero a Scheraggio – deren Name von einem in der Nähe fließenden Kanal, in den man den Müll abließ, herrührt – verbleiben nur wenige Spuren. Vom Eingang des Uffizienmuseums ist es möglich, einige Überreste des Mittelschiffs und der Apsis zu sehen. Auch vom Anfang der Via della Ninna, sieht man würdevolle Steinsäulen, die das Mittel- vom linken Schiff teilen. Zwischen diese Säulen wurde eine Gedenktafel aus Marmor gestellt, um an Dante und Boccaccio zu erinnern, die in der S. Piero a Scheraggio-Kirche das Wort bei öffentlichen Debatten nahmen.

S. Piero a Scheraggio (lato esterno da via della Ninna)

Die Sammlung der Zeichnungen und Drucke

Die Sammlung der Zeichnungen und Drucke füllt das ganze ehemalige alte Medici-Theater aus. Es handelt sich um eine großartige Kollektion von ca. hundertviertausend Exemplaren. Begründer dieser Sammlung war der Kardinal Leopoldo dei Medici, ein leidenschaftlicher Kollekteur, der seine Schätze dem Enkel, Granduca Cosimo III°, überließ. Im Laufe der Zeit wurden immer mehr Werke hinzugruppiert und -gesammelt. Erinnern wir nur an die vom Großen Prinzen Ferdinando hinterlassene Erbschaft, oder an den Kauf der Francesco Bartolozzi-Stiche und der über zwölftausend Zeichnungen reichen Santarelli-Sammlung. Dieses unermeßliche Vermögen hatte bis zum Anfang des 20. Jahrhunderts keine angemessene Unterbringung; oft wurden die Zeichnungen und Drucke willkürlich in der Uffiziengallerie ausgestellt, vor allem im Corridoio vasariano, wobei man eine große Gefahr in Bezug auf ihre Erhaltung einging. Erst Corrado Ricci, zu jener Zeit Museumsdirektor, trug alle Drucke und Zeichnungen zusammen, ordnete sie und rief so die heutige Kollektion, das Gabinetto, ins Leben.

Pontormo: Disegno

Pontormo: Testa Virile

Leonardo: Disegno

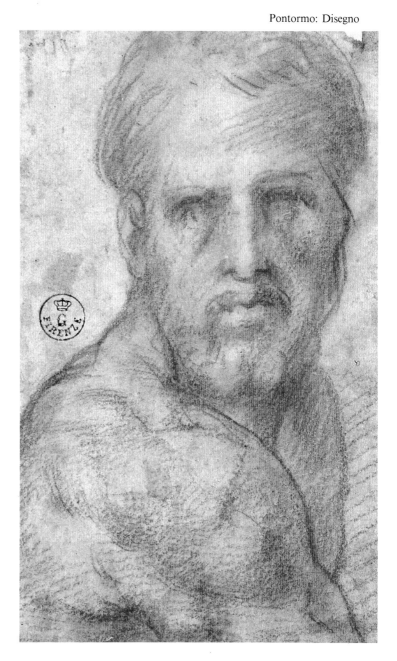

7

The Sculptures of the Uffizi

The Uffizi was first conceived as a museum of antique and modern sculpture. In the course of the centuries the palace commissioned by Cosimo and designed by Vasari increased its collection to include archaelogical pieces, epigraphs and statues of all periods. It wasn't until the 19th century that the administrators decided to reduce the enormous collection and transfer all the medieval and modern sculptures to the Bargello and many classical works to the Archaeological Museum. Thus the Uffizi only exhibits part of the Medici sculpture collection. These sculptures are used mostly as decoration for the museum's three galleries and represent both in quantity and quality a remarkable panorama of Greek, Hellenistic and Roman art.

In the left wing (on the entrance side) is Hercules Slaying the Centaur, *a Hellenistic statue restored by Giovanni Caccini in 1585; a sarcophagus of the late Roman period; an Attic statue representing the god of health; the statue of an athlete; a sarcophagus with Phaedra and Hippolytus, classic example of the Roman funerary art of the 3rd century; a sarcophagus with bas-reliefs illustrating the abduction of the daughters of King Leucippus and a marriage which Castor and Pollux attended, a Roman copy of a Greek original;* Proserpine, *also a Roman copy of a Greek original; a bust of Nero of black basalt; a sarcophagus with scenes of Meleager hunting the Calydonian wild boar, a Roman copy a Greek original;* Hercules; *the* Sarcophagus of the Muses, *Roman copy of a Greek original of the 5th century B.C.;* Pan and Daphne; Attis, *Roman work of the Imperial period.*

In the smallest part of the corridor, the part that connects the main wings of the museum, there are several important statues, including the Head of a Dying Giant, *copy of an original of the 2nd century B.C.; the* Bust of Antinoös, *late Imperial period; the* Bust of Homer, *of black basalt;* Ceres; *the* Statue of a Woman, *Roman art; the* Altar with the Sacrifice of Iphigenia, *Greek art, 1st century B.C.; a Roman sarcophagus of the 2nd century with the fall of Phaëthon;* Minerva; Venus; *and, finally, a beautiful Hellenistic statue representing a seated girl.*

In the right hand corridor the visitor can admire other examples of classic art, amongst which are the Discobolus; *the* Bust of Cicero; Leda and the Swan, *Roman copy of a Greek*

Copia romana da originale ellenistico: Lo Spinaro

original; Dionisus with a young satyr, *Roman copy of a Greek original;* Nereid riding a sea horse *and* Apollo Citharoedus, *once again Roman copies of Hellenistic sculptures. If we continue along the corridor we find the* Laocoön, *one of the many modern copies of this*

Sculture del II Corridoio

Sculture del II Corridoio

statue (16th century), by Baccio Bandinelli. And further on, a Bust of Caracalla and the statue of an injuried warrior, a typical example of the Roman art of the 3rd century B.C. In addition to the sculptures exhibited in the gallery – of which we have mentioned just a few – the Uffizi has dedicated one room, Room n° 1, to classic art. It is located at the beginning of the 1st gallery and contains many remarkable examples of the Greek and Roman bas-relief.

Scultura del II Corridoio

der Galerie stehen die Caracallabüste *und die Statue eines verletzten Kriegers, typisches Beispiel der römischen Kunst des 3. Jahrhunderts vor Christus.*

Außer den in der Galerie ausgestellten Skulpturen, von denen wir nur einige aufgeführt haben, widmen die Uffizien der klassischen Kunst einen Saal (Nr.1).

Die Wandteppiche

In den Uffizien sind zahlreiche und bedeutungsvolle Wandteppiche ausgestellt, viele davon florentinischer Herkunft. Es war Cosimo

I., der in der Hauptstadt seines Staates eine Wandteppichfabrik entstehen ließ. Absicht des Prinzen war, das Prestige und die Ökonomie der Stadt wieder in Schwung zu bringen, wobei er auf das künstlerisch-handwerkliche Gewerbe zielte, eine Kunst, die Florenz kaum kannte. Cosimo wirkte wie gewöhnlich in großem Stil: er ließ bekannte flämische Künstler, wie Roost und Karcher, kommen und gab ungeheure Summen für die Wandteppichherstellung aus. Die Bemühungen des Prinzen wurden nicht enttäuscht; aus den florentinischen Manufakturen kamen richtige Meisterwerke, wie die von Bachiacca entworfenen Wandteppiche oder

Arazzo

I Corridoio

Werke des Stradano, welche Jagdszenen darstellen.

Der größte Teil der Wandteppiche, die in den Uffizien aufbewahrt werden, sind mehr oder weniger aus Dekorationsgründen, zusammen mit den klassischen Statuen, in den langen Korridoren der beiden Hauptflügel ausgestellt. Im linken Teil des Museums findet man u.a.: Wolfsjagd *und* Wildschweinjagd, *ausgeführt von Squilli nach einem Entwurf des Stradano;* Groteskenwandteppiche *und* Jahresmonate, *Stoffe, die von flämischen Handarbeitern, nach Zeichnungen des Bachiacca, ausgeführt wurden;* Hoffeste von Enrico von Frankreich und Caterina Medici, *die in Brüssel auf Anordnung des französischen Hofes, wahrscheinlich nach Zeichnungen des Quesnel, angefertigt wurden. Später, als Christina di Lorena den Ferdinando I. der Medici zur Hochzeit geleitete, wurden der jungen Braut diese Kunstwerke geschenkt und so nach Florenz transportiert.*

Weitere Wandteppiche findet man im gegenüberliegenden Teil der Galerie. Hier hängen Stücke von Gaspare Papini, nach Entwürfen von Alessandro Allori, die Teil der Christuspassionsserie *bilden. Dann findet man noch die ausländischen Handarbeiten, die biblische Theme behandeln und Schlachtszenen darstellen.*

Arazzo di scuola fiamminga: Caterina de' Medici e Enrico III

The Uffizi Gallery

Layout of the second-floor rooms

A. The Uffizi Vestibule with some altars, Greek and Roman busts
B. The Vestibule to the Gallery with Roman statuary
C. First Gallery
1. Archaeological Room
2. Thirteenth Century and Giotto
3. The Sienese fourteenth century
4. The Florentine fourteenth century
5-6 International Gothic
7. The early Renaissance
8. The Filippo Lippi Room
9. The Antonio del Pollaiolo Room
10-14. The Botticelli Room
15. The Leonardo Room
16. The Map Room
17. The Hermaphrodite Room
18. The Tribune
19. The Perugino and Signorelli Room
20. Dürer and the Germans
21. Giambellino and Giorgione
22. The Flemish and German masters
23. The Correggio Room
24. The Miniatures Room
D. Second Gallery
E. Third Gallery
F. Stairway leading to the Vasari Corridor
25. Michelangelo and the Florentines
26. Raphael and Andrea del Sarto
27. Pontormo and Rosso Fiorentino
28. The Titian Room
29. The Parmigianino Room
30. The Room of the Emiliani
31. The Dosso Dossi Room
32. Sebastiano del Piombo and Lorenzo Lotto
33. The Corridor of the Sixteenth century
34. The Veronese Room
35. Tintoretto and the Barocci
H. The exit hallway
41. The Rubens Room
42. The Niobe Room
43. The Caravaggio Room
44. The Rembrandt Room
45. The Eighteenth-century Room
I. The Terrace of the Signoria Loggia
L. The Uffizi 'Bridge'
M. The Palazzo Vecchio (Town Hall)

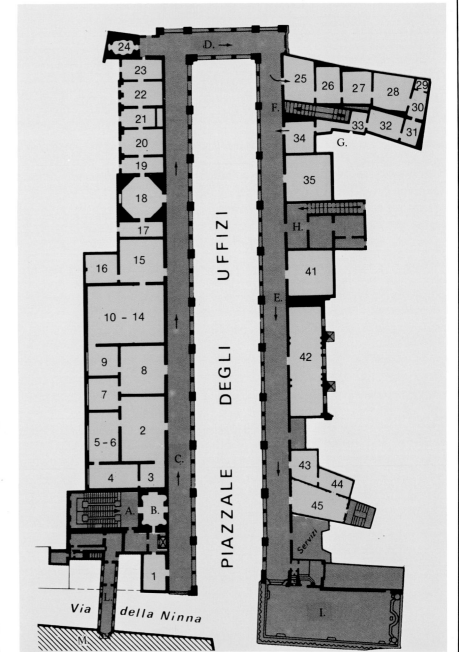

Giotto

«This great man was born in 1267 in the villa at Vespignano, fourteen miles from the city of Florence. His father, known as Bon-done, was a simple worker of the soil». *Thus Vasari begins his description of Giotto, about whom we know very little. In fact, even his date of birth is uncertain, probably in 1267, although the date of his death is known to us*

Giotto: Madonna in trono

Maler seiner Zeit werden ließ. Nach Vasari war er dazu verdammt, den Spuren seiner in ihrem dürftigen Bauernleben verwurzelten Eltern zu folgen. Jedoch entdeckte der damalige Maler Cimabue in Giotto einen Künstler und nahm ihn mit sich nach Florenz.

Nach einer wahrscheinlichen Romreise begab sich Giotto nach Florenz, wo er das Kruzifix (heute in Santa Maria Novella) und die Madonna für die Ognissanti-Kirche schuf. In Padua malte er zwischen 1304 und 1308 den Freskenzyklus über die Geschichten der Jungfrau. Die Allerheiligenmadonna, auch nach Ghiberti ein Werk Giottos, wird von der Kritik für ein ausgesprochenes Meisterwerk gehalten. Das für die Ognissanti-Kirche ausgeführte Altarbild stellt die Madonna mit Kind auf dem Thron dar. Zu Füßen der Madonna befinden sich Engel und Heilige, deren Anwesenheit auf den Namen der Kirche und somit auf alle Heiligen anspielt. Das Gemälde ist unter die von Assisi und Padua einzureihen, da Giotto sich hier von der byzantinischen Malerei loslöst, um an den Plastizismus der klassischen Kunst anzuknüpfen. Dadurch entstand die großartige Abbildung der Madonna, deren Gesicht durch ein leichtes Lächeln und durch verschwommene helle Farben sehr sanft erscheint. Die schon in der antiken Kunst bekannte dritte Dimension weiß Giotto auszunutzen. Das geht eindeutig aus der geschickten Perspektive des Throns hervor, der in eine Räumlichkeit gestellt ist, die fast als Wirklichkeit erscheint – dank auch der Abbildung menschlicher Figuren auf beiden Seiten der komplexen architektonischen Errichtung.

Cimabue

Cenni di Pepo, auch Cimabue genannt, lebte in Florenz zur Zeit des Dante und war einer der berühmtesten Künstler des 13. Jahrhunderts. Über sein Leben haben wir wenig Notizen und unsicher ist auch das Geburtsdatum, welches Vasari als 1240 angibt.

Cimabue stellte einen bedeutenden Fortschritt in der Evolution der mittelalterlichen Kunst dar, da er eine noch priesterliche, unbewegliche und byzantinische Kultur zu befruchten und anzuspornen wußte. Diese Erneuerungen fanden ihre volle Reife in der Kunst Giottos'. Wichtige Momente für das künstlerische Wachstum von Cimabue waren die Reisen nach Assisi und Rom. Während er in Florenz den Einfluß der dramatischen Spra-

Cimabue: Madonna in trono   Bonaventura Berlinghieri: Dittico

che von Coppo da Marcovaldo – mit dem er in San Giovanni zusammenarbeitete – erfahren hatte, kam er in der Ewigen Stadt mit dem Sinn der Klassizität in Kontakt, der die alte kaiserliche Hauptstadt nie ganz verlassen hatte.

Mit der Madonna von Santa Trinita löst sich Cimabue von der Starrheit der byzantinischen Kunst. Es hinterbleiben noch einige Elemente der Ikonenmalerei, vor allem in der segnenden Geste des Kindes; im Vergleich zu den vom Maler eingeführten Neuerungen haben diese Elemente jedoch eine zweitrangige Bedeutung. In der symmetrischen Struktur des Bildes füllt Maria den Mittelteil aus; schon alleine diese Figur löst sich von der Tradition und wir stehen nicht mehr einem unkörperlichen Bild gegenüber, sondern einer konkreten und realen Person. Die Mutter Jesus' sitzt auf einem Thron vielseitiger architektonischer Stilwendungen, der mit Intarsien und Edelsteinen geschmückt ist und von einem Engelschor umgeben wird. Die eindeutigste Neuerung des Malers ist – durch eine perspektivische Anordnung der Engel und durch die Konstruktion auf unterschiedliche Höhen des Thrones –, die dritte Dimension zu erreichen. Eine Theorie über die Perspektive gab es noch nicht und die Fluchtlinien des Thrones wurden noch auf zufällige Art erdacht; in seiner Gesamtheit aber, existierte der Sinn für die Tiefe schon.

Duccio di Buoninsegna: Madonna in trono

Duccio di Buoninsegna

Die Kenntnisse vom Leben des Duccio di Buoninsegna sind äusserst gering. Er wurde um 1255 in Siena geboren und starb in derselben Stadt gegen 1319. In Siena, wo er in der Contrada del Laterino wohnte, schätzten ihn seine Mitbürger sehr. Diese allgemeine Achtung wird von seinem erfolgreichen Meisterwerk bezeugt: La Maestà (die Majestät). Als 1311 die große Tafel beendet wurde, feierten sie die Sieneser durch Jubel- und Lobkundgebunden. Duccio wurde für seine Arbeit gut belohnt; so kostete die Maestà die Auftraggeber 2000-3000 Goldgulden, eine bemerkenswerte Summe, die nicht zuletzt wegen des enormen Gebrauchs von edlem Metall für die Ausführung zu rechtfertigen ist. In den Uffizien wird eine große und wichtige Tafel von Duccio aufbewahrt: die Madonna Rucellai.

Die Madonna Rucellai ist eine Wasserfarbentafel großer Dimensionen: 4,5 m hoch und 2,9 m breit. Das Bild wird durch einen großen Goldrahmen, den Duccio selbst angefertig hat, geschützt. Auf dem Rahmen, innerhalb kleiner Kreise, sind dreißig Heilige porträtiert, darunter «San Pietro Martire». Das Bild zeigt eindeutige Gemeinsamkeiten mit der Madonna di Santa Trinita von Cimabue auf; tatsächlich erinnern die Aufstellung der Figuren und ihre Gesichter an die Tafeldes florentinischen Meisters; diese Ähnlichkeiten jedoch enden schon hier: im Werk Duccios' treten schon die typischen Merkmale der sienesischen Malertradition – so verschieden von der florentinischen – in Erscheinung. In der zweiten Hälfte des 13. Jahrhunderts gab es in Siena auf der einen Seite den Geschmack für die neo-byzantinische Malerei, auf der anderen entdeckte man durch den französischen Miniaturkodex die Gotik.

Simone Martini: Annunciazione

Simone Martini

Simone Martini, one of the most important Sienese painters of the 14th century, was born in 1284 and died in 1344. Ghiberti wrote that «Simone was a very noble and very famous painter. The other Sienese artists held him to be the best...». *His reputation soon crossed the borders of his home town and Simone was called to work in many other Italian cities. In school of painting, based on reality, and preferred the fairy-tale, refined world of Gothic art, with its gentle, diaphanous figures set against dazzling golden grounds.*
The Annunciation *at the Uffizi is another of Martini's great works. This large*

(1.84 x 2.10 m) tempera on wood was painted in 1333 for the cathedral of Siena and placed on the altar of Saint Ansano. In 1799 the Grand Duke Pietro Leopoldo decided that this masterpiece was to enrich the Uffizi collection and had it transferred to the Florentine museum.
Not all of the Annunciation *is the work of Simone Martini: the two lateral figures which are said to represent Saint Margaret and Saint Ansano betray the hand of Martini's brother-in-law, Lippo Memmi. The central panel, though, is a typical product of Simone's art. It is full of gothic elements, and the spacious effects conquered by Giotto have almost disappeared. Except for the throne, there*

Piero Lorenzetti: Polittico scomposto

are no architectural constructions to provide perspective. And even the marble pavement, devoid of geometrical shape, helps to diminish the painting's depth. The figures are typically Gothic. Giotto's sculptural treatment is totally absent, and the Angel and Mary are incorporeal, ethereal bodies, elegant and aristocratic looking but a bit cold. Notice the study of attitudes: the perplexity and reserve of the Virgin, her modesty and circumspection which contrasts with the fieriness of the Angel shown kneeling in front of her, suddenly still after flight. In its exquisite elegance the painting is reminiscent of the feudal homage given by knights to their mistresses and seems to have been influenced by courtly literature.

Pietro Lorenzetti

Pietro Lorenzetti was born in Siena about 1280 and carried out his activity in several Italian cities. In Assisi he had the opportunity to see Giotto's work at first hand and the great Florentine master's art left an indelible mark on him. Later we find him working in Florence and Siena. In his native town, Pietro executed his last works: the Nativity of the Virgin for the cathedral of Siena and the frescoes for the facade of Santa Maria della Scala (now lost) on which he worked with his brother Ambrogio. Pietro died in 1348 from the terrible Black Death, the plague that Boccaccio described in the Decameron, which

N. Ser Sozzo Tegliacci: Madonna con Bambino

raged over Europe and Italy. Siena was badly struck by it and both Pietro and his brother Ambrogio fell victim to its fury.
The Uffizi houses two paintings by Pietro Lorenzetti: the Madonna Enthroned with the Child and Angels *and the* Altarpiece of the Beata Umiltà. *The first work, a tempera on wood, portrays Mary on the throne with the Child and surrounded by angels. This painting is remarkable not only for its beauty but*

also for the number of interesting elements it presents.
In the Altarpiece *we notice the same synthesis of Giottesque Florentine elements with the Sienese feeling for colour. This complex work portrays the* Beata Umiltà, *who died in 1310, at the centre of the painting; eleven side panels illustrate various scenes from her life. At the bottom of the altarpiece Lorenzetti painted seven small, round portraits of Christ, two pious women and several saints. At the top there were once four cusps with the Evangelists and their symbols, but only those of Saint Luke, Saint Mark and Saint John are to be found at the Uffizi.*
The figures that fill the altarpiece are all Giottesque in their treatment. Notice, for example, the last panel on the right where the body of the Beata is surrounded by a crowd of people: the figures are conceived as volumes and are defined by a line which almost seems to incise each individual mass. On the other hand, every scene of this typically Florentine painting presents the Sienese love of colour, which makes the castles, landscape and interiors look as if they were set in a fairy-tale world.

Ambrogio Lorenzetti

Ambrogio Lorenzetti was born in 1285 at Siena and died of the plague in his native town in 1348. He is one of the most interesting panters of the 14th century. According to Vasari «Ambrogio was a skilled colourist of frescoes and he used tempera with great ability and ease». Lorenzetti worked in Florence for a long time and there his art was held in great esteem. His continuous artistic relations with the city of Giotto ended up by exerting a deep influence on his style: absorbing the elements of the great master, Lorenzetti's figures became more plastic, like true-to-life characters with well-defined volume. In spite of the lesson he learnt from Giotto, Ambrogio always remained close to the Sienese tradition, with its feeling for colour and the fairy-tale elegance of the Gothic world. His frescoes on the Effects of Good and Bad Government in the City and the Country *are a classic example of his art. These masterpieces, painted in the Sala dei Nove at the Palazzo Pubblico of Siena, illustrate in their poetic, but lively and realistic images what everyday life was like in the late Middle Ages.*

Ambrogio Lorenzetti: Quattro storie di S. Nicola

The most important of Lorenzetti's works exhibited at the Uffizi in the Scenes from the life of Saint Nicholas of Bari, *painted for the church of San Procolo.*
The work is composed of two panels in tempera painted about 1330. The diptych did not arrive at the Uffizi until 1919. Each wing is divided into two sections with illustrations of the main events in the life of the saint. Thus each of the four sections illustrates a different scene: Saint Nicholas giving a dowry to three young women of humble origin, Saint Nicholas being named Bishop of Myra, Saint Nicholas resuscitating a child killed by the Devil and Saint Nicholas saving Myra from a famine.

Although Ambrogio does not have the Florentine master's decisiveness in using perspective, he is nonetheless able to convey the idea of depth, above all through a wise distribution of chiaroscuro in the complicated maze of walls, balconies, crenellations and columns. His feeling for colour is great, and always linked to the modelling of solid human figures. Take the last scene as an example. The love of detail and feeling for colour are obvious, the atmosphere hovers between dream and fantasy, but the people in the scene the inhabitants of Myra who went with the saint to receive the Byzantine grain merchants are real, concrete men. Their volume in clearly defined it is almost tangible.

Bernardo Daddi: Madonna con Bambino e Santi

Giottino

We know very little about the life of Giotto di Mastro Stefano, known as Giottino. The Lives of the Artists *is one of the few sources we have for this Florentine painter, although Vasari often confuses him with Maso di Banco. According to the great Renaissance architect, Giottino was born in 1324 and died of consumption in 1366; he is supposed to have led a humble and secluded life as his introverted and melancholy nature dictated. But, as mentioned above, Vasari's facts may not be accurate, especially those referring to the date and the cause of Giottino's death, for he generally confuses Giottino with Maso di Banco. It seems likely that the painter, son of master Stefano, achieved a certain success*

Agnolo Gaddi: La Crocifissione

Maestro della S. Cecilia:
S. Cecilia e storie della sua vita

Giottino: Pietà

during his short lifetime and that he also worked outside Tuscany, especially in Rome and Assisi.

A follower and imitator of Giotto's painting, Giottino never forgot the experiences of the Sienese Gothic artists nor did he remain indifferent to those of the northern Italian painters. The Pietà, considered to be his masterpiece, was painted for the church of Saint Remigio between 1360 and 1365 and has been on exhibit at the Uffizi since 1851. This tempera on wood (1.95 x 1.34 m.) is one of the most beautiful examples of 14th century Italian art.

The San Remigio Pietà is truly a magnificent work of art. It portrays a number of figures on different planes, set against a gold ground with the symbols of the Passion and the Redemption. The sculptural treatment of the figures clearly derives from Giotto's art, but the artist's feeling for colour is rather special. These colours are often bright and luminous and they help to identify the figures whose attitude and expression has been carefully wrought. Notice, for example, how differently sorrow manifests itself on the faces of the Holy Women and those of the Saints farthest from the central scene.

Gherardo Starnina: La Tebaide

Gherardo Starnina

According to Vasari, Gherardo di Jacopo Starnina, known as Starnina, was born in Florence in 1354. A precocious child who at a very young age had shown a marked disposition for fine arts, he was apprenticed at the workshop of Antonio Veneziano and there he learned to draw and paint admirably. Also according to Vasari, Starnina's first commission in Florence was for the frescoes of the Castellani Chapel in Santa Croce, where he portrayed scenes from the life of Saint Anthony and Saint Nicholas.

In the Uffizi we find an extremely beautiful painting by Starnina: the Thebaid, *one of the few works by this master not to have been lost. For a long time it was attributed to other, more famous painters, like Fra Angelico and Paolo Uccello.*

This panel measures 0.80 x 2.16 m and was probably commissioned by a religious order. It portrays a monastic community founded by Saint Pancratius in about the 4th Century at Tabennesi, a locality of Thebes of Egypt. This painting reflects the influence of the frescoes painted by Lorenzetti on The Effects of good and bad Government in the city and in the country. *It is divided by a complex rocky landscape into well-defined spaces with scenes of monastic life.*

Lorenzo Monaco

Lorenzo Monaco, called Piero di Giovanni before he entered a Florentine monastery, was born at Siena in 1370. Even before he abandoned the lay world, he attained a considerable reputation for his work which stylistically is reminiscent of Angelo Gaddi and Spinello Aretino. In 1390 at the age of twenty he entered the convent of Santa Maria degli Angeli and thereafter was known as Lorenzo Monaco.* In the convent he began to cultivate miniature painting and within a few years he became the most prestigious exponent of the famous Angioli school which produced such exquisite works as the Antifoniano *of 1394 and the* Corale 8 *of 1400, both of them preserved at the Biblioteca Laurenziana of Florence. But painting remained his favourite activity during all his lifetime and he continued to execute magnificent works until his death in 1423.*

In the Uffizi we can admire two masterpieces by Lorenzo Monaco: the Coronation of the Virgin *and the* Adoration of the Magi. *The* Coronation *is a polyptych (4.50 x 3.50 m) painted in 1414 for the church of the Convento degli Angeli. The artist has represented the subject in the traditional manner, with Christ placing the crown on Mary's head amidst a group of angels and saints. Lorenzo's style is*

Lorenzo Monaco: Incoronazione della Vergine

a product of the artistic tendencies of his time and therefore is closely related to the International Gothic. The slender figures have been painted with rapid, graceful strokes and stand out against a golden background, a lingering 14th century element. The artist has chosen his colours with great ability: the differing shades of yellow, green, light blue and white, all bright colours, create luminous effects of remarkable beauty. But equally important is Lorenzo's feeling for decoration and detail, two elements derived from his schooling in miniature painting. Nevertheless, despite the Gothic elements, Lorenzo has a very special manner, one which makes him different from all the other artists

*«Monaco» = monk, friar.

23

Gentile da Fabriano: Adorazione dei Magi

Gentile da Fabriano

Gentile di Niccolò, known as Gentile da Fabriano, was born in the town of Fabriano in the Marches in 1370. We know very little about his life: it is likely that he was trained in the Umbrian and Sienese schools and that there he came into contact with a number of artisans, goldsmiths and illuminators whose style was closely related to the Gothic tradition.

The Adoration of the Magi *is articulated on a number of planes that embrace a vast scenario which is crowned in the background by lordly residences fortified with towers. At the foot of the castles a long procession of riders returning from the hunt unwinds along the hilly landscape. This setting takes us back to the courtly and refined world of high of flam-boyant Gothic. The same subject is repeated in the foreground with the group of riders accompanying the three Kings. Here there are also a group of horsemen dressed in rich brocades and damasks, steeds with elaborate, precious harnesses, greyhounds and squires. The three princes from the Far East face the Holy Family and render hommage to the Saviour: they represent the three ages of man. The centre of the painting is occupied by the youngest King, the image of the perfect gentleman. Notice how carefully the artist has drawn this key character: his blond hair is carefully dressed, his gestures are controlled as a perfect gentleman's should be; his precious clothing is brocade and gold; and a squire helps the prince fix his spurs, a sign of nobility and chivalresque dignity.*

Beato Angelico: Incoronazione della Vergine

Fra Angelico

Guido di Pietro, who has gone down in history by the name of Fra Angelico, was born at Vicchio di Mugello near Florence in about 1400. At the age of 17 he was already successful as a painter and illuminator by preference close to the International Gothic style. Six years later, in 1423, Guido entered the convent of San Domenico at Fiesole and having abandoned the secular world and embraced the ecclesiastical one he changed his name to Fra Giovanni, and is mentioned by that name in the documents of the time.

Fra Angelico is a very important painter: his art exerted deep influence on the following generation of painters: on Domenico Veneziano e Piero della Francesca, for example. He succeeded in embracing and applying Masaccio's discoveries, and Masaccio's perspective became part of his art, although Fra Angelico always remained in the religious sphere which transcends the material, everyday world.

Paolo Uccello: La battaglia di S. Romano

The most important work by Fra Angelico exhibited at the Uffizi is the Coronation of the Virgin, a tempera on wood (1.12 x 1.14 m) painted about 1435 for the Florentine church of San Egidio and acquired by the museum only after World War Two. This painting shows how Fra Angelico used the discoveries of his century to extol Christianity and create religious propaganda. Let's take a close look at the painting's composition: the scene has a certain depth resulting from the decreasing height of the figures that surround the central episode of the Coronation. The faces of the saint, the Apostles and the Angels clearly evince a feeling of peace and joy. The whole is bathed in a blinding light which illuminates the profiles and the clothes; from the musical instruments comes the sound of joyous and jubilant melodies. The idea that peace and happiness come to mankind only through religion is clearly implicit in Fra Angelico's painting; the artist used the elements of Masaccio's new artistic vocabulary in order convey this deeply pious message.

Paolo Uccello

Paolo di Dono, known as Paolo Uccello, was born in 1397. His father Dono di Paolo, a barber and surgeon at Pratovecchio, in the Casentino, did not become a Florentine citizen until 1373. Young Paolo began by learning the profession of goldsmith: in fact, he was apprenticed at Ghiberti's workshop at the time when the Florentine artist was working on the first door of San Giovanni. Shortly thereafter Uccello began to paint, and in 1425 he journeyed to Venice where he worked as a master mosaicist in the Cathedral of San Marco. On his return to Florence he gained a reputation as a great artist and also acquired the nickname of Uccello (bird). According to Vasari, it was due to the fact that Paolo loved to paint animals and all sorts of birds. In 1445 he left Florence for a while and went to Padua, where he had been called by Donatello.

His major work, however, remains the Rout of San Romano, three panels commissioned by Cosimo de' Medici and painted between 1456 and 1457.

This large tempera (1,82 x 3,23 m) is an exceptional example of Paolo's art. The battle is portrayed as a horrifying clash where men, animals and arms are tangled in a gory brawl. Terrified horses, broken lances, robot-like riders, crossbows, helmets and scimitars are all active participants in a highly dramatic scene in which the thrust of each against the other seems suddenly frozen. But in spite of its highly dramatic tones the Rout of San Romano *is pervaded by a fantastic, almost fairy-tale atmosphere. In fact, the landscape in the background with its ploughed, hedged fields and charging animals, the unreal colours and the soldier participants in a chaotic, frightful tourney all contribute to give this episode of war an abstract, surreal tone.*

Masaccio

Tommaso di Ser Giovanni di Mone Cassai, known as Masaccio, was born at Castel San Giovanni (now San Giovanni Valdarno) on the 21st of December 1401. His father, a notary by profession, died when Masaccio was only five years old. A few years later his mother, Jacopa di Martinozzi, married an apothecary. Young Masaccio left his home town and moved to Florence, as the big city offered many opportunities for success to an artist who was starting out in painting; furthermore there he knew another artist from Valdarno, Mariotto di Cristofano, who was married to one of his half sisters and who had been working in Florence since 1419. In 1422 Masaccio registered at the "Arte dei medici e degli speziali" (the doctors' and apothecaries' guild) and it is probably then that he began to practice his profession in the city. There are a number of famous works from that period: in 1424 he painted the Madonna and Child with Saint Anne and Angels *and started to paint the frescoes in the Brancacci Chapel. A year later he moved to Rome where he worked on the* Snow Polyptych *at the Church of Santa Maria Maggiore, and in 1426 he travelled on to Pisa. In spite of the numerious commissions he received Masaccio was always short of money.*

The Madonna and Child with Saint Anne and Angels *is the only work by Masaccio exhibited at the Uffizi. The painting measures 1.75 x 1.03 and was executed about 1424 for the Church of Sant'Ambrogio in Florence. The figures of the Virgin and Child are attri-*

Masaccio: Madonna e S. Anna

buted to Masaccio, while Saint Anne and most of the angels were painted by Masolino da Panicale. Masaccio's figures have the compact, plastic qualities of a sculptural group:Through a skilled use of chiaroscuro and perspective, Mary and Jesus lose all signs of courtly abstraction, and become solid, concrete, full-bodied figures. They are so immersed in an atmosphere of truth and reality that their figures are almost tangible. The dicovery of this new dimension was of fundamental importance and opened up new possibilities for all the painting of subsequent years, making Masaccio an indispensable point of reference for entire generations of painters.

* Tommaso ß «Tommasaccio». The suffix «-accio», in Italian, means bad, careless, vulgar.

CLARVS INSIGNI VEHITVR TRIVMPHO ·
QVEM PAREM SVMMIS DVCIBVS PERHENNIS ·
FAMA VIRTVTVM CELEBRAT DECENTER ·
SCEPTRA TENENTEM

Piero della Francesca

Piero Della Francesca

Piero della Francesca was born between 1410 and 1420 in the town of Borgo San Sepolcro. His father Benedetto de' Franceschi was a humble tanner and shoemaker; of his mother Romana Pierino we know only that she was born in Montevarchi.
Very little is known about the first years of Piero's life: he was probably instructed in the fundamentals of painting by a local master and at about the age of 15 decided to go to Florence to perfect his style.

The Uffizi has in its collection the Portraits of Federico di Montefeltro, Duke of Urbino and of His Wife. *This diptich is composed of two panels which measure 47 x 33 cm. each, and are painted with tempera on both sides. They portray in profile, the Lord of Urbino Federico da Montefeltro and his wife Battista Sforza. The painter's emphasis on detail clearly shows the influence that Flemish painting exerted on his style. The profiles are set against an airy, remote landscape which melts into the horizon beneath a limpid sky: these are the lands over which the Duke and*

Piero della Francesca: Federico da Montefeltro

Duchess exercise their absolute power. On the reverse of the panels Piero painted the triumphs of both characters.

Domenico Veneziano

Domenico di Bartolomeo, known as Domenico Veneziano, was born in Venice in the beginning of the 15th century. In 1438 we find him in Perugia where he painted several frescoes in the houses of the Baglioni family. From the Umbrian town Domenico wrote to Piero de' Medici asking him for work in Florence.

The Uffizi houses a very important work by Veneziano: The Madonna and Child with Angels, *known also as the* Santa Lucia dei Magnoli Altarpiece. *This large tempera on wood (2.09 x 2.13 m) represents the Virgin Enthroned with the Child and Saints Francis, John the Baptist, Zenobin and Lucy. The first thing to look at in this painting is the artist's palette. The soft, extremely delicate colours, – with rose predominant –, imbue the scene with a gentle atmosphere. Only the figure of John the Baptist, clearly inspired by Andrea del Castagno, wears a tunic of bright red: it is Veneziano's sole concession to the lively*

Domenico Veneziano

tones so popular in northern Europe. The soft colours are modulated by the play of morning light which settles discreetly on the figures and the complex Renaissance architecture framing the sacred subject. Another fundamental element is the confident use of perspective, firmly established during Veneziano's Florentine experience. This painting of an interior is tangible proof of the fact that his early empiricism made way for precise mathematical relationships which enabled the painter to succeed in creating third dimension effects.

The Filippo Lippi Room

Filippo Lippi:
Incoronazione della Vergine

Filippo Lippi:
Madonna col Bambino e due angeli

Filippo Lippi

Filippo Lippi was born in Florence in 1406; his family lived on the left bank of the Arno, in the quarter of Ardiglione not far from the church of Santa Maria del Carmine. His father Tommaso Lippi, a butcher, died when Filippo was two years old; his mother had died a little before that, probably soon after giving birth to Filippo. Orphaned of both parents, the boy was placed in the care of a paternal aunt, a women named Lapaccia, who raised him until her impoverished condition forced her to turn the boy over to the convent of Santa Maria del Carmine; Thus, still a child, Filippo found himself in a Carmelite convent. There he studied painting, drawing his inspiration from the powerful figures that Masaccio had executed in the Brancacci Chapel.

After becoming a famous painter it is likely that Lippi worked for a while in Padova, though he carried out most of his activity in Florence where his work is documented from 1437 on. In the Tuscan city Lippi enjoyed the Medici's protection and could dedicate himself exclusively to his art despite his religious habit. It seems that his being a friar did not stop him from having several love affairs, for he was a very sensual man. In the «Lives» Vasari gives a description of this trait of the artist's personality: «It is said that he was so amorous that when he saw a woman who pleased him he would have given all he pos-

sessed o have her...

Amongst the many works by Lippi at the Uffizi, there are two particularly famous ones: the Coronation of the Virgin *and the* Madonna and Child with Angels. *The first painting is a large (2 x 2.87 m) tempera on wood painted between 1441 and 1447 for the church of Sant'Ambrogio. This painting was inspired in part by the one that Fra Angelico had painted a few years before on the same subject. But the nature of the two paintings is very different: notice how carefully Lippi places his figures in exact perspectival position and how the light coming down from above creates special chiaroscuro effects on their faces. The figures are portrayed with great abundance of details and their expressions are vary greatly, even though in most cases they are dominated by a subtle strain of melancholy. Notice, at last, the Carmelite friar in the left foreground – – it is one other than the painter himself!*

The Madonna and Child with Angels *is another of Lippi's masterpieces. This small tempera on wood was painted about 1445. It measures 0.95 x 0.62 m. Tradition has it that the face of the Madonna is that of Lucrezia Buti, the woman loved by the painter. This exquisite work foreshadows, both in the gentle, melancholy expression of the Virgin and the landscape of the background, a number of elements later to be absorbed by the great Florentine artists of the second half of the 15th century, from Botticelli to Leonardo.*

Alessio Baldovinetti: Annunciazione

Vecchietta: Madonna e Santi

Il Vecchietta

Lorenzo di Pietro, known as il Vecchietta, was born at Castiglion d'Orcia in the Sienese countryside, about 1410. In his youth he moved to Siena and in 1428 he was already registered in the artists' guild. In time he developed a type of painting that combined Gothic elements with other typically Early Renaissance elements derived from Florentine art.
The Madonna and Saints *is the only painting by il Vecchietta at the Uffizi. It was painted in 1457 for Giacomo di Andreuccio Petrucci. This panel reflects the influence of the Gothic style, which lingered on in 15th century Siena. The figures' solemn attitude is particularly obvious in the blessing gestures of Mary and Child. Notice the static posture of the figures and the gold background against which they are set: these two elements contrast sharply with the Renaissance theories which in those very same years began to flourish and produce art of great new splendour.*

Alessio Baldovinetti

Alessio Baldovinetti was born in 1425 in Florence. He never left his home town and died there in 1499. A pupil of Fra Angelico, Baldovinetti later absorbed the influence of various artists, including Domenico Veneziano, Piero della Francesca, Andrea del Castagno and Paolo Uccello. Baldovinetti was inspired by their example, as evidenced by his careful handling of perspective and his inclination for spacious and airy settings. But he also remained close to the Florentine tradition and organized his works around precise and careful designs.
Amongst his most famous works let us mention the Nativity *of the Chiostro Piccolo at the church of SS. Annunziata in Florence, a* Madonna *now at the Louvre and the decoration of the Chapel of the Cardinale del Portogallo at the church of San Miniato a Monte in Florence.*
The Uffizi exhibits two interesting works by Baldovinetti: Madonna and Child with Saints

and the Annunciation. *The latter work was painted about 1447 at a time when the painter was absorbed in his studies of perspective. Notice how carefully he constructed the beautiful open gallery with its classic round arches and its slender columns. Behind* *the portico, to give more depth to the scene, Baldovinetti placed some trees, Their each and every detail painstakingly described. This emphasis on detail is also evident in the clothing and attitude of the two elegant and refined figures.*

Antonio del Pollaiolo

Antonio Benci was born in Florence in 1431. His father Jacopo sold chickens and other poultry and it was this fact that earned young Antonio and his younger brother Piero the nickname of Pollaiolo.

Antonio began working as a goldsmith at Bartoluccio Ghiberti's workshop and after a short time his remarkable talent came to light. Bartoluccio's stepson, Lorenzo Ghiberti, noticed the boy's talent and employed him as his assistant on the doors of San Giovanni. Vasari wrote that when Antonio was set to work on a festoon there, «...he made a quail which can still be seen, so fine and perfect, that it lacks only the power to fly».

The Uffizi exhibists two small paintings on wood by Antonio del Pollaiolo: Hercules and the Hydra *and* Hercules and Antaeus, *paintings which have an adventurous story in common. They were stolen from the museum during World War II and given up for lost, but in 1963 they were found in Los Angeles and twelve years later they were brought back to Florence.*

Hercules and the Hydra *(17 x 12 cm) was painted about 1470 and represents the struggle between the hero – symbol od Florence –and the many-headed monster. The scene is pervaded by an extreme violence with the adversaries are tensed in the terrible and supreme effort of battle, a tension also reflected in the expression of exasperation the hero's face. The vast landscape in the background contrasts sharply with this furious scene: serene and harmonious, it lies beneath a pure and limpid sky.*

The same elements appear in the second painting, Hercules and Antaeus, *(16 x 9 cm), executed a few years after the first one. This painting also represents a fierce, savage mythological scene. Notice how skillfully the painter has rendered the strained muscles of the figures, under the tremendous stress, how he has highlighted the dramatic expression on the faces of the opponents. Antaeus, held back by Hercules' steel embrace, explodes in a cry of derperate pain, a last act of rebellion against the violence to which he is submitted. The hero expends all his physical and psychological reserves to achieve this difficult victory.*

Antonio del Pollaiolo: Ercole e Anteo

* «pollo», *in italian, means chicken.*

Antonio del Pollaiolo: Ercole e Idra

S. Botticelli: La Fortezza

Piero del Pollaiolo: La Prudenza

Piero del Pollaiolo

Piero Benci, known as Pollaiolo, was born in Florence about 1441. He often worked together with his more famous brother, Antonio del Pollaiolo. The Pollaiolo brothers collaborated so closely in their works that it is often difficult to distinguish Antonio's hand from Piero's. Nevertheless the latter's work is marked by a lesser strength, a weaker composition and opaque, lifeless colour.

Antonio e Piero del Pollaiolo: S. Vincenzo, Giacomo e Eustachio

Piero del Pollaiolo died in Rome in 1496. Several of his works are housed at the Uffizi, the most important of which are the Six Virtues. *These six temperas on wood were painted between 1469 and 1470 for the Arte della Mercanzia (merchants' guild) as decoration for the Council Chamber.* Faith, Hope, Charity, Prudence, Justice *and* Temperance *are symbolized by six nearly identical young women seatted on intricately shaped and richly decorated thrones.*

Jacopo del Sellaio

Jacopo del Sellaio was born in Florence in 1442; he spent all his life in his native town and died there in 1493. He was a pupil of Botticelli's, but also absorbed the influence of other masters, including Ghirlandaio. Although successful, Jacopo was a minor artist who dedicated himself mainly to decorating chests: the Adoration of the Magi, *now part of the Kress collection in Memphis, is dis-*

Jacopo del Sellaio: Convito della Regina Vasti

S. Botticelli: Adorazione dei Magi

*played on such a chest. His most valuable
work, however, is the* Crucifixion *at the
church of Santa Maria a Cestello in Florence:
in it he achieves the particularly dramatic
effects which are usually alien to his gracefull
narrative style.*
The Uffizi houses one of his paintings, the
Banquet of Ahasverus, *a tempera on wood
that was once part of a chest. This painting
evidences the artist's skill in illustrating a
little-known biblical episode with great viva-
city and a wealth of detail.*

S. Botticelli: Giuditta e Oloferne

Sandro Botticelli

Alessandro Filipepi was born in Florence in 1445. Mariano, his father, was a humble tanner, but in spite of his modest situation he wanted Sandro to study and apprenticed him to a very famous artist, Fra Filippo Lippi. At the age of twenty Sandro – known to everyone as Botticelli, perhaps because his brother was nicknamed "Il Botticello" – was already an official painter of the Medici court. In 1475

he completed a standard full of symbols and allegories for Giuliano de' Medici, who carried it in the famous tourney in Santa Croce later immortalized by Agnolo Poliziano's verses. A few years later Sandro demonstrated his affection for the Lords of Florence by portraying the most important members of the powerful Medici family in an Adoration of the Magi, *painted between 1476 and 1477 and now exhibited at the Uffizi. In this work we can recognize Cosimo the Elder, Piero the*

S. Botticelli: La Calunnia

*Gouty, young Lorenzo the Magnificient and the painter himself, in a yellow robe among the group of figures to the right in the foreground. In 1478 the artist was commissioned by Pierfrancesco de' Medici to paint the fa-*mous Allegory of Spring (La Primavera), *although some art historians date the work to 1482. The year 1478 was a dramatic one for Florence: the Pazzi family plotted an attempt on the life of Lorenzo the Magnificient and his brother Giuliano, and the latter was*

stabbed to death by the conspirators in the Cathedral of Santa Maria del Fiore. Sandro Botticelli was shocked and afflicted by the tragic event that burst in upon the serene, cultivated Neoplatonic Medici circle to which he belonged.
Three years later the famous painter, was called to Rome and there he painted Moses and the Daughters of Jethro *and the* Punishment of Core *in the Sistine Chapel. But the artist never adapted to the Roman milieu with*

S. Botticelli: Madonna della Melagrana

its controversies and envies; so a year later he returned to Florence. This was one of the happiest periods of Botticelli's life: in 1482, shortly after arriving home, he painted the Madonna del Magnificat *and* Pallas and the Centaur, *both in the Uffizi. Later the artist* concluded another masterpiece: Mars and Venus, *now at the National Gallery, London, a painting full of allegorical meanings, like the artist's preceding works. In 1484 Botticelli reached the climax of his career with* The Birth of Venus, *a work commissioned from*

S. Botticelli: Annunciazione

him by Lorenzo di Pierfrancesco.
At the end of the century Botticelli was over-come by a moral, existential and religious crisis, which was due to the death of Lorenzo il Magnifico and the ensuing political chaos and also to the inflamed preaching of Gerola-mo Savonarola. His late works clearly reflect the anguish and fears that held him in their grip. Moral scruples led him to accept com-missions only for religious and ethical works. From this period date the Pietà (Munich), The Allegory of Slander (Uffizi) and the

S. Botticelli: Allegoria della Primavera

Botticelli: La Primavera (part.)

Nativity *(National Gallery), all three works pervaded by a strong feeling of anxiety clearly evidenced in the figures' dramatic attitudes. This great painter died on the 17th of May 1510 and was buried in the church of Ognissanti. At the time of his death his fame, glorious as it had been just a few years earlier, had vanished almost completely, partly* because Michelangelo, Leonardo and Raphael made Botticelli's art seem a thing of the past.
Let's now turn to the two most famous masterpieces by Botticelli at the Uffizi: The Allegory of Spring *(La Primavera) and the* Birth of Venus.
According to some art historians the Allegory

S. Botticelli: Nascita di Venere

was painted in 1478 while others set its date four years later in honor of the marriage of Lorenzo di Pierfrancesco and Semiramide Appiani. This beautiful painting has become the symbol of the cultivated humanistic Florentine milieu, delighting in Classical antiquity and impregnated with Neoplatonism. The beautiful figure of Venus, symbol of Humanitas, occupies the centre of the painting; on her right are the three Graces and Mercury dispersing the clouds. To the left Zephyr grasps Flora and the latter, fecundated by the god, strews flowers on the ground.

The Birth of Venus was executed some years later. This large tempera on wood (1.72 x 2.78 m) was commissioned from the artist by Lorenzo di Pierfrancesco for his villa at Castello. This painting, like the aforementioned one, is a great and learned allegory. Venus is chaste and pure, despite her nudity, the symbol of the Humanist philosophy which with its cult of nature has come to benefit and improve the world. Notice the emotional tension and marked melancholy of the faces of the beautiful female figures: they hint at the anxiety and restlessness that accompanied not only the painter but also the refined Humanistic world in which he lived.

Domenico Ghirlandaio: Madonna in trono e santi

Domenico Ghirlandaio

Domenico di Tommaso Bigordi, known as Ghirlandaio, was born in 1449. Little is known about the beginning of his career, though it is likely that he was apprenticed to Alessio Baldovinetti; Ghirlandaio is one of the most important and prolific artists of the Italian Quattrocento. He was especially gifted as a fresco painter and used this technique in a number of his works, such as those in the Cathedral of San Gimignano and in the Churches of Santa Trinita and Santa Maria Nuova in Florence. In his frescoes he portrayed the rich Florentine bourgeoisie dressed in sumptuous clothes and wearing ostentatious jewelry. Ghirlandaio was a skilled inter-preter of patrician family taste: the Sassetti, the Vespucci and the Tornabuoni were all among his clients. His detailed narrative style was especially suited to describe the costumes and atmosphere of his time, and as early as the Vespucci Chapel fresco at the Church of Ognissanti (1472-73) his great skill as a portraitist appears. This youthful work shows a plastic strength and unified design reminiscent of Verrocchio and Pollaiolo, two artists whom he probably got to know at the beginning of his career.
Amongst his last works, the most interesting are a number of famous portraits: the Old Man and the Child, *(the Louvre),* Giovanni Tornabuoni, *now at Lugano, and the* Adoration of the Magi *in the Uffizi, similar in*

Domenico Ghirlandaio: Adorazione dei Magi

composition to Botticelli's painting of the same subject.

The famous Florentine museum also houses the Madonna and Child with Angels and Saints, *a work painted about 1490 which arrived at the Uffizi in 1853. In this painting, Ghirlandaio seems indebted to Verrocchio, especially in the figures of the Virgin and Child. The linear tension gives Mary poised-for-flight attitude, held back only by the position of the arms and the bust. The sculptural treatment of the Virgin's face gives it a pre-*

cious quality, as if it were made of hard stone. These elements – which are also found in the cherubim and in the archangels Gabriel and Raphael – are less obvious in Saint Zanobi and Saint Justin, the two kneeling figures depicted in a more decorative manner. Nevertheless the total scene is rich in sumptuous details: the carpet and vase of flowers in the foreground, the panel decoration of the pavement and the open air portico in the background with cypresses and orange trees behind.

Filippino Lippi: Adorazione dei Magi

Filippino Lippi

Filippino Lippi was a son of the arts: he was born in 1457 of the turbulent relationship of Filippo Lippi and the nun Lucrezia Buti. Filippino was orphaned at the age of twelve. Before his death, his father had placed him in the care of a friend of his, Fra Diamante. After learning the fundamentals of painting from Fra Diamante, Filippino found himself another, more interesting teacher: Sandro Botticelli, whose style was to influence Filippino to a great extent. Having attained a certain reputation, Lippi began to work almost exclusively in Florence, where he painted the frescoes of the Brancacci Chapel in the church of Santa Maria del Carmine and executed several paintings on wood for churches, religious and private institutions. In 1483 he left Florence for Rome and there he worked in the Caraffa Chapel at Santa Maria sopra Minerva.

H. Vander Goes: Trittico Portinari   Filippino Lippi: Madonna col Bambino

Filippino was a very popular man in Florence; his funeral was a solemn one and was attended by many people who showed their sorrow over his death: «...Filippo was buried ... in S. Michele Bisdomini ... and while they were carrying him to burial all the shops of Via de' Servi were locked up, as is done at the funerals of men of eminence». The Uffizi houses many works by Filippino Lippi. Some of these works – like the Self-portrait *and the* Portrait of an Old Man – *are only attributed to him, while others, like the* Adoration of the Child, *are certainly his and extremely famous. The most important, however, is the* Adoration of the Magi, *a large oil on wood measuring 2.58 x 2.43 m.*

This painting can be examined from many points of view, especially with regard to its influences. Despite a few details extracted from Botticelli – for example, the young prince kneeling in front of the Virgin – the overall style looks ahead to the 16th century, especially to the art of Leonardo da Vinci. In addition, it reflects the influence of northern European art, introduced into Florence through the works of Hugo van der Goes. The Flemish vision clearly appears in the feeling for landscape, with nature described in great detail and exotically dressed figures moving about in the background, accompanied by fairy-tale objects and animals.

Hugo Van der Goes

Hugo van der Goes was born in Ghent in 1440. In 1468 he was called to Bruges and there he was commissioned to execute the pageant decorations and scenes for the wedding of Charles the Bold and Margaret of York. During those years he also painted his first important works – amongst them the Original Sin *and the* Deposition, *now in Vienna. In Bruges he met Tommaso Portinari, an agent for the Medici, who commissioned him to paint a triptych for the Florentine Church of Sant'Egidio: thus the* Portinari Altarpiece *was born. It was a work which upon arrival in Florence received much praise and later exerted a strong influence on Tuscan art of the period. The figures of Portinari and his family are portrayed on the wings of the triptych, a very strongly modelled work, full of a plastic energy uncommon in Flemish art.*

In the center of the triptych is the Virgin kneeling in front of the Child: the shepherds, the angels and Saint Joseph are placed in such a way that they create almost a circle around the Redeemer. The work has a complex symbolic intent which today is very difficult to reconstruct. According to some critics the 15 angels represent the 15 joys of the Virgin.

Leonardo: L'Epifania

Leonardo da Vinci

Leonardo, the great universal genius, was born in 1452 at Vinci, a small town near Florence. He was the illegitimate son of a well-to-do notary named «Ser Pietro». In 1469 his father took him to the Tuscan capital and apprenticed him to Andrea del Verrocchio. Leonardo's remarkable talent was immediately noticed and appreciated and three years later he was officially registered at the Florentine painters' guild. The Baptism of Christ, *painted together with his master, and the* Annunciation *belong to this period. In the* Baptism, *Leonardo's early mastery is revealed in the background, the figure of Christ and especially the angel on the left, a figure that roused admiration and surprise in many Florentines. His other youthful works were painted soon thereafter: the* Benois Madonna, *now in Leningrad, the* Madonna of the carnation *(Munich) and* Saint Jerome *(Pinacoteca Vaticana).*

In the summer of 1482 Leonardo left Florence for the first time and entered the service of Lodovico il Moro in Milan. There he was appointed to the prestigious charge of painter and engineer to the Duke; and he executed daring projects for hydraulic systems, war machines and industrial fortifications.
Leonardo's pictorial oeuvre is not a very large one, as a result of both his varied interests and his extreme desire for perfection. The Uffizi has reserved two very interesting and extremely beautiful youthful works of Leonardo.
The Annunciation, *an oil on wood, was painted between 1472 and 1475. It was first attributed to painters like Verrocchio and Ghirlandaio, but eventually art historians definitively assigned it to Leonardo. The figures in the painting have extremely gentle features and their faces show an obvious melancholy that harmonizes with the landscape in the background, a misty and remote scene derived from the art of northern Europe. The*

Leonardo da Vinci: Annunciazione

Verrocchio: Battesimo di Cristo

influence of Flemish art is also evident in the paintstaking delicacy of execution of the dresses, which are complicated and carefully studied in every detail.
The other work at the Uffizi – the Adoration of the Magi *– is less traditional and presents a number of innovative elements. Commissioned from Leonardo by the monks of San Donato at Scopeto in 1481, this large painting (2.43 x 2.46) was never finished because the painter, a year after he began it, left Florence for Lodovico il Moro's court. It is, as has been said before, an unconventional work, for it is completely lacking in the elements of a typical adoration scene: the three kings, the shepherds, the angels, Saint Joseph, the grotto. Mary and the Child occupy the center of the panel and they are surrounded by a circle of highly individualized, dramatic looking figures. Further away in the background, rocks and ruins, wild horses, exotic trees and other elements help to create an atmosphere of extreme psychological tension, centered on the Child and the mother. It is almost as if the artist wanted to symbolize the hope of peace, serenity and salvation that humanity places in the figure of Christ.*

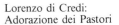

Piero di Cosimo:
Immacolata Concezione

Piero di Cosimo

Piero di Lorenzo was born in Florence in 1461. His father, a goldsmith by profession, sent young Piero to learn the art of painting at the workshop of Cosimo Rosselli. The maestro became a second father to the boy to such a point that little by little he became known as Piero di Cosimo. Solitary and introverted but gifted with an exceptional imagination, he was Rosselli's favourite student and chosen by his maestro as his assistant for the frescoes he painted at the Sistine Chapel. When Cosimo died Piero started working indipendently and attained immediate success, but he also became increasingly solitary and strange.

In spite of his unusual personality, full of phobias and idées fixes, Piero became the favourite painter of many private clients, who commissioned chests, paintings on mythological subject and devotional works.

Piero never left Florence except for a youthful trip to Rome. He died suddenly in 1521. It seems that the last years of his life were tormented by a continuous trembling of the hands which rendered every activity extremely difficult.

The Uffizi houses a famous painting of Piero di Cosimo, Perseus liberating Andromeda. *A work of his maturity, this oil on wood reflects the influence of Leonardo and Raphael and some critics have seen in it a sensibility close to Mannerism. Notice the fairy-tale landscape (according to the legend it was situated on the coast of Ethiopia) with its golden hues that shine under the bright clear sky. Vasari wrote in his Lives:* «The landscape is very lovely and the colours are soft and graceful, harmonious and well-blended. Piero finished the work with the greatest care».

Lorenzo di Credi

Lorenzo di Credi was born in Florence in 1459. He received his artistic training at Verrocchio's workshop and once his apprenticeship was finished he began to study the works of other painters of his day, amongst them Perugino, Leonardo and the Flemish artists. In his youth he was a versatile painter, capa-ble of fulfilling commissions of all types, from devotional to profane.

The Adoration of the Shepherds *at the Uffizi is one of his most famous works. This painting on wood was completed in 1510 for the church of Santa Chiara; it evidences the artist's great technical skill, especially in the execution of the figures inspired by those of Leonardo and Verrocchio.*

Hans Memling

Hans Memling (Stoccarda)

Hans Memling was born at Seligenstadt in 1435. He studied under Rogier van der Weyden in Brussels. In 1465 he settled in Bruges where he had great success as a painter and portraitist. He died in 1494 at the age of fifty nine. Memling was a cultured and refined man devoid of existential anguish and religious doubts: his compositions are calm and serene, and he achieved his best results in his altarpieces and portraits.

Amongst his most famous works we should mention the Tryptych of Women *(National Gallery, London),* Saint Benedict *(Uffizi), the* Annunciation *(Lehman Collection, New York),* Bathsheba in the Bath *(Stuttgart Museum) and the portraits of* Tommaso Portinari *(Metropolitan Museum, New York) and* Benedetto Portinari *(Uffizi). In the Uffizi we can admire another work of Memling: the* Madonna enthroned with the Child and two Angels. *This small painting is quite remarkable for its abundance of details, the throughtful and serene expression of the figures and the beautiful northern landscape in the background.*

17 The Hermaphrodite Room

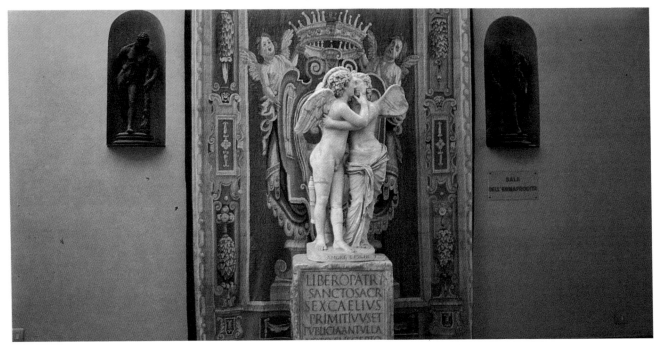

Tribuna del Buontalenti

A. Allori: Bianca Cappello

Alessandro Allori

Alessandro Allori (1535-1607) was born and lived all his life in Florence. He received his training at Bronzino's workshop and he tried to combine his master's art with Michelangelo's monumentality and Raphael's colour. A famous, sought-after artist, after 1570 he became the official painter of the Medici court and carried out his activity at the Palazzo Vecchio, in the Uffizi and at the Villa of Poggio a Caiano.

The Portrait of Bianca Cappello, *exhibited at the Florentine Gallery, was executed by the artist after 1560. Bianca Cappello was a member of the Venetian nobility and mistress to the Grand Duke Francis I. In 1579, she became his legal wife. The portrait has been masterfully executed; notice the skilled use of light, an element of primary importance in the painting, as it sets off the beautiful oval-shaped face of the powerful courtesan.*

A. Allori: Venere e Cupido

Franciabigio: Madonna col Bambino

Giorgio Vasari: Lorenzo il Magnifico

Giorgio Vasari

Giorgio Vasari was born at Arezzo in 1511 and began to paint at the age of thirteen. He received his training in Florence and lived there until he moved to Rome in 1531. In the Eternal City he had the opportunity to study at first hand the works of Michelangelo and Raphael and to deepen his already vast knowledge. In addition to this he found an illustrious and powerful patron in Cardinal Farnese, thanks to whom he received his first important commission: the frescoes of the Palazzo della Cancelleria.

In 1550 Vasari published the Lives of the Painters, Sculptors and Architects, *a series of important biographies that have been and continue to be indispensable source for the history of art.*

Franciabigio

Francesco di Cristofano, known as Franciabigio, was born in Florence in 1482 and died while still a young man in 1525. At the beginning of his career he was a pupil of Piero di Cosimo; later he broke with his master and opened up a workshop with Andrea del Sarto, with whom he worked at the Villa of Poggio a Caiano. He painted the Annunciation *(Pinacoteca, Turin) and* The Wedding of Mary *(Church of SS. Annunziata) and he frescoed part of the Chiostro dello Scalzo in Florence. The* Madonna *and child with Saint John is one of Franciabigio's most beautiful paintings. Notice how the painter, an exponent of the Tuscan Mannerist School, has used some of the typical elements of Raphael's and Michelangelo's art.*

La Tribuna: Busto di Francesco I de' Medici

La Tribuna (esterno)

A. Bronzino: Eleonora da Toledo con il figlio Giovanni

Bronzino: Ritratto di Francesco de' Medici

Luca Signorelli e Pietro Perugino: Crocifisso

Perugino

Piero Vannucci, known as Perugino, was born about 1448 at Città della Pieve. His style developed under the influence of Piero della Francesca and Verrocchio, who was his teacher in Florence between 1470 and 1472. Soon he became a famous and sought-after painter who in his works succeeded in uniting the perfect design of Verrocchio's school with

Perugino:
Ritratto di Francesco delle Opere

the vast, light-filled landscapes of Piero della Francesca's works. His popularity was not only limited to Florence, for he was called to work in many Italian cities: Rome, Lucca, Bologna, Venice, Cremona, Milan, Ferrara, the Marches and Perugia. In Perugia he painted the Polyptych of Saint Peter *and at the end of the 15th century he completed the frescoes of the Collegio del Cambio. During this perod Perugino had amongst his pupils the young Raphael, who after a short time broke away from the master's style and tried to find more personal and less mannered solutions.*

Perugino painted a great number of his works in Florence: the Crucifix *of Santa Maria No-*

vella and the portraits of Don Biagio Milanesi *and* Baldassare Monaco *in the Monastery of Vallombrosa are only a few. In 1492 he completed the* Christ *in the Garden for the Church of San Giusto, and this, like the preceding portraits, now in the Uffizi Gallery. The Florentine museum also acquired, in 1784, one of Perugino's masterpieces: the* Madonna and Saints, *a work which originally hung at the Church of San Domenico in Fiesole.*

The painting measures 1.78 x 1.64 m. and was executed in 1493 during one of the most productive periods of the artist's career. Although his inspiration was to diminish over the years, Perugino continued painting until the day before his death, at Fontignano in 1523. The Madonna and Saints *focuses on a rigorous respect for balance and symmetry: a number of figures are arranged according to a rigid symmetrical scheme within a space limited by complex architectural constructions. Notice the extreme sculptural treatment of the figures: their lines are sharp and well defined, their volume and mass are well specified in the best Florentine tradition, probably a result of Verrocchio's teachings. The vast and luminous landscape, on the other hand, is reminiscent of the backgrounds of Piero della Francesca, an artist who played a definitive role in Perugino's artistic training.*

Perugino: Giovinetto

Melozzo da Forlì: Annunziata

Melozzo da Forlì

Melozzo degli Ambrosi was born at Forlì in 1438 and died there in 1494. A pupil of Piero della Francesca, he worked in Rome where in 1477 he painted the fresco of Sixtus IV appointing Platina prefect of the Vatican Library. *Three years later he executed several frescoes in the Roman church of SS. Apostoli. Afterwards he worked in the Basilica of Loreto and the Church of San Biagio at Forlì. The two paintings by Melozzo exhibited at the Uffizi are a rarity: in fact, the painter centred his activity on frescoes, and rather large ones too. The* Angel *and the* Virgin of the Annunciation *were part of the door of an organ that was later dismantled. We must also point out that on the reverse of the* Angel *panel there is a portrait of Saint Presdocimo.*

Luca Signorelli

Luca Signorelli was born at Cortona in 1450. According to Vasari, Signorelli received his training in Arezzo under Piero della Francesca: « Luca Signorelli, an excellent painter ... was a pupil of Piero of Borgo a San Sepolcro and in his youth he made a great effort to equal and even to surpass his master. While he was working in Arezzo with his master and living with his uncle Lazzero Vasari ... he imitated Piero's style so well that it was difficult to perceive any difference between them ».
Signorelli's youthful works, dated about 1480,

Luca Signorelli: Predella della Trinità

Luca Signorelli: Sacra Famiglia

are clearly indebted to Piero della Francesca's paintings. The Flagellation, *the* Madonna and Child *(Brera) and the* Circumcision *(National Gallery, London) evidence the conflict between Piero's luminous, open style and the linear tension and scientific naturalism of Pollaiolo. The synthesis of the two becomes line here becomes intensely dramatic: contours are sharply defined and the individual figures stand out in an incredible way.*
In the Uffizi we can admire a number of Signorelli's works including the Crucifixion of Mary Magdalene *and the* Trinity with Virgin and Saints.
The Crucifixion is considered to be a late work of Signorelli: it was probably painted in the early 16th century. In this painting Sig-

norelli combines elements derived from Florentine culture with other typically Flemish ones. The plants at the feet of the crosses and the macabre touch of the lizard emerging from a skull were recurrent details of the art of northern Europe, although they had already been adapted to the artistic idiom of Florentine painters in the second half of the Quattrocento. Notice the plasticity of the secondary figures, clearly reminiscent of Pollaiolo's style, here completely assimilated into Signorelli's late vision. The figure of Christ is also taut and vibrant, while Mary Magdalene is equally tense as she turns open-mouthed to look at the Lord. The landscape and monumental ruins are painted in hushed tones and dotted with light yellow at some points.

Francesco Francia:
Evangelista Scappi

Luca Signorelli's Trinity *was commissioned by the Confraternita della Trinità dei Pellegrini in Cortona. In the upper part of the panel is the Holy Trinity, with the Virgin and the Child at the centre, the Archangels Michael and Gabriel to the sides and Saints Augustine and Anthony below. Despite their static poses, these figures are drawn with a clear, tense and vibrant line that endows them with a particular energy. The top of the painting seems more archaic, with the Trinity surrounded by a halo of light and the faces of cherubim.*

Francia

Francesco Raibolini, known as Francia, was born in Bologna about 1450 and died there in 1517. His early painting was influenced by the art of the school of Ferrara; later he absorbed some typically Tuscan elements and finally he arrived at a moderate classicism.
The Uffizi exhibits the Portrait of Evengelista Scappi. *It was executed by Francia when he had already made a name for himself and had developed a classically restrained style.*

Albrecht Dürer: Adorazione dei Magi

Albrecht Durer

Albrecht Durer was born in Nuremberg in 1471. The son of a well-to-do goldsmith, young Albrecht began his training as a draughtsman in his father's workshop and was later apprenticed to a woodcut illustrator named Michael Wolgemut. About 1490, the year in which he painted the Portrait of his father *which is now in the Uffizi, Durer began to travel. The desire to see new places and to study the artistic experiences of others was to remain a constant throughout the life of this versatile genius in architecture, graphics, and art theory as well as painting.*

In 1494 Durer set out on his first journey to

Italy, anxious to see the art of the Reinassance at first hand. He settled in Venice, but travelled quite often to other northern Italian cities. He was most impressed by the works of Mantegna and Giovanni Bellini, although Leonardo also influenced him. As a result of the new notions he had acquired, the German master broke away from the lingering Gothic tradition and adopted a typically Renaissance style. In 1505 he felt once more the desire to return to Italy. During this second journey he also dedicated most of his time to Venice but he visited other cities as well – – like Bologna, where he probably came into contact with Michelangelo. In 1507 he returned to Germany: his conquest of the Renaissance had come to an end as he possessed all the elements he needed to introduce the Italian experience into his country.

Back in Germany he resumed his work with great energy: in 1526 he painted the Four Apostles, *two panels which he later willed to his native town of Nuremberg. He died in 1528, honoured by everyone as a great artist. In addition to the aforementioned* Portrait of his father, *the Uffizi Gallery exhibits several other works by Durer: the* Adoration of the Magi, *the* Madonna of the Pear, *the* Great Passion, Saint Philip the Apostle *and* Saint John the Apostle.

The Adoration of the Magi *is the most interesting of the Uffizi works. It is an oil on wood which measures 0.99 x 1.35 m. and was painted about 1504, in a period when Durer was still young, but had already come into contact with Italian art and as a result had overcome many of the "gothifying" elements typical of his early work. Notice the perfection of the figures, depicted with great abundance of detail, the interest in perspective and the feeling for landscape, certainly derived from the artist's Flemish experience.*

A. Dürer: Ritratto del padre

Hans Von Kulmbach: Storie dei Santi Pietro e Paolo

Hans Von Kulmbach: Storie dei Santi Pietro e Paolo

Lucas Cranach the Elder

Lucas Cranach was born in Kronach in 1472. Before his thirtieth birthday he left his home town and settled in Vienna where he gained a considerable reputation for his paintings and etching. Over the years he developed an increasingly pictorial language, whose most outstanding characteristic was the aura of mysticism and enchantment surrounding his landscapes, an element which would later become typical of the Danube School.

In 1505 Cranach was appointed court painter to the Elector of Saxony, Frederick the Wise. In the meantime he had become quite famous and the number of commissions he received had increased. In order to fulfill the great demand the Germain painter, showing an uncommon business sense, set up a large workshop where he employed a number of helpers and assistants so well-trained that it is almost impossible to distinguish Cranach's mature work from the work of the members of his shop.

Amongst the subjects preferred by the artist

and his assistants were portraits of the Lords of Saxony and of the fathers of the Reformation to which Lucas had sincerely adhered. In addition, he painted a number of frescoes of hunting scenes in the castles of Austria and, by continuously developing the fabulous aspects of his art, he arrived at a cultured and refined Mannerism.

Cranach died at Weimar in his eighties, in 1551. His immense oeuvre, so varied in subject and technique, had earned him a leading position amongst the German painters of his time.

The Uffizi exhibits several works by Cranach. But many of them cannot be attributed to the artist himself, for they betray the hand of the assistants employed in his workshop. Such is the case, for example, of the portraits of Martin Luther, Melanchton, Johannes I, Elector of Saxony *and* Frederick III the Wise, Elector of Saxony.

The two large paintings of Adam and Eve *(1.72 x 0.63 and 1.67 x 0.61 m respectively) were executed by Cranach himself. These panels were painted in 1528 and for a long time they were attributed to Durer, in spite of*

Lukas Cranach il Vecchio:
Martin Lutero

the fact that their style is the exact opposite of that of the painter from Nuremberg. Durer felt an almost religious respect for the proportions of the human figure as well as for perspective and the sculptural treatment of bodies, all elements which are foreign to Cranach's world. In fact the figures of Adam and Eve are elongated out of all proportion, and the colouring and poses are extremely unnatural. In spite of this, the figures possess charm and elegance, as well as a certain subtle, though obvious, ambiguity and a marked sensuality in the case of Eve. The figures are set against a dark background, giving the composition an archaic tone: and this tone is in fact one of the characteristic elements of Lucas Cranach's artistic production.

Jan Brueghel il Vecchio:
Il grande calvario

Jan Brueghel the Elder

Jan Bruegel the Elder was born in Brussels in 1568 and died at Antwerp in 1625; he was the second child of the famous Pieter known also as the "Peasant Brueghel". Jan followed in his father's footsteps and studied painting under Pieter Goetkint. After visiting many European cities he settled in Antwerp and there opened his own studio. Jan Brueghel's oeuvre consists mostly of landscapes, mythological and allegorical subjects. He showed a marked preference for still lifes with flowers and this earned him the nickname of "Brueghel of the flowers".

Brueghel the Elder's work exhibited at the Uffizi is a rather faithful copy of Durer's Great Passion *which is also on display at the Florentine gallery.*

G. Bellini: Allegoria sacra

Giovanni Bellini

Giovanni Bellini was born in a family of artists. His father Jacopo, was a famous painter who had been a pupil of the renowned Gentile da Fabriano: his older brother was official painter of the Venetian Republic and as such had travelled with the doge to Constantinople where he had painted a portrait of the Sultan. His sister was married to Andrea Mantegna, whose style would exert a deep influence on Bellini's artistry. The biography of this great master is a very simple one. He was born in Venice in 1432 and in his early youth he began to work in his father's workshop; there he learned to create form and colour similar to that of the Late Gothic tradition. After 1460 he broke away from this old-fashioned style and got closer to the great art of Mantegna. However, within a few years, Bellini's originality began to show through: the more intimate nature of his paintings, pervaded by a tangible melancholy, and the increasingly clear relationship established between human figure and landscape were to become two elements of primary importance in his art. Nature becomes one with man, reflecting his feelings and Psychological condition, and there is a complete transfiguration of the Divine, which becomes the protagonist of the artist's works as nature. At the summit of his career Bellini completed such magnificent works as the Blessing Saviour *(Louvre), the* Pietà *(Galleria di Brera, Milan), the* Pesaro Altarpiece, *and the* Grief over the Dead Christ *(Pinacoteca Vatican). By 1500 Bellini had become a famous artist and the official painter of the Venetian Republic. He then decided to incorporate a number of innovations into his style, perhaps in response to the competition presented by new artists from the younger generation. Sensitive to every message, the aging Giovanni succeeded in partially transforming his artistic language, although he never abandoned his favourite subjects. During this last phase of his career he created several masterpieces including the* Madonna of the Meadow *(National Gallery, London) and* Venus with the looking glass *(Kunsthistorisches Museum, Vienna) Bellini*

Vittore Carpaccio: Alabardieri e Anziani

continued to paint until he reached a very advanced age: he died in 1516, old and famous, at the age of 84.

The Uffizi exhibits three works by Bellini: the Grief over the Dead Christ, a beautiful monochrome tempera full of stifled pain and deep melancholy, the Portrait of a Young Man and the Sacred Allegory.

This last painting is undoubtedly one of his most famous works. The Sacred Allegory was concluded in the last decade of the 15th century. It is not a large canvas, measuring only 0.73 x 1.19 m, but in spite of its size it charms the observer with a mysterious fascination. The allegorical meaning of the work is still completely unknown. On a terrace of beautiful polychrome marble we see the Holy Family surrounded by a number of Saints; the rest of the painting is occupied by a vast landscape, probably the surrounding of a lake or a river. The water, mysterious and captivating with its opaline reflections, unwinds in wide bends within a rupestrian landscape stippled with fortresses, animals and mythological and human figures. The composition is saturated with a mysterious air, not only because of its subjects but also because of the fabulous symbolism which permeates every detail. The human figures, the architectural constructions, the rocks and hills have an almost metaphisical value and seem to convey occult messages to the observer.

Giorgione

Zorzon or Giorgio, known as Giorgione, was probably born about 1478 at Castelfranco Veneto. About his private life we know only that he was born into a modest family: the lack of documents doesn't allow us to reconstruct his biography with any real certainty. It is known, though, that in his early youth he went to Venice, where he opened the doors to his varied interests and cultivated poetry and music as well as painting. A cultured and refined follower of the Humanist philosophy, he was influenced by the art of Antonello da Messina and, to a certain extent, Giovanni Bellini and Leonardo.

The Uffizi exhibits two small painting on wood by Giorgione, both of which were probably executed about the beginning of the 16th century. The first painting represents the trial of fire which Moses had to go through in his childhood as a punishment for having stepped

Giorgione: Mosè
alla prova del fuoco

on the Pharaoh's crown. This subject is an unusual one and shows the author's solid cultural background. As in many of his other works the background landscape is vast and its natural and architectonic elements have already acquired the plasticity typical of the artist's style.

The Judgement of Solomon *is also a remarkably interesting panel, quite different from the first, especially in Giorgione's technique. The reason lies in the fact that the* Judgement *was executed at a later date and some of the details – especially the draperies and the clothes – betray the hands of his pupils. The artist reserved a large part of the composition for the natural elements which recede along successive planes before melting into the horizon. Cliffs, trees, prairies, villages and mountains all succeed in creating a delightful landscape which, despite its apparent tranquility, encloses in its bosom a disturbing message filled with mysterious meaning.*

Albrecht Altdorfer

Albrecht Altdorfer was probably born about 1480 and died in 1538. He is one of the most interesting German painters of the early 16th century. Altdorfer's art, influenced by the "Danube School", has protoromantic elements. The artist's fervid imagination created fabulous, dramatic compositions, filled with rich landscapes and arcane, disturbing, even terrifying figures. Landscape is a major element in all of Altdorfer's paintings, to the point that it prevails over subject. Amongst his most famous works are: The Battle of Alexander, Silvan Landscape, Birth of the Virgin *(all at the Alte Pinakothek, Munich) and the* Landscape with a satyr and his family *(Staatlichen Museen, Berlin).*
The Uffizi exhibits two paintings by Altdorfer: The Martyrdom of Saint Florian *and the* Saint Florian's departure. *Both works are typical examples of the German master's art for they show his feeling for landscape and are pervaded by a sense of enchantment.*

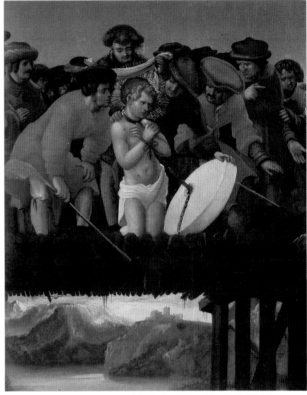

Altdorfer: Martirio di S. Floriano

Hans Holbein il Giovane: Sir Richard Southwell

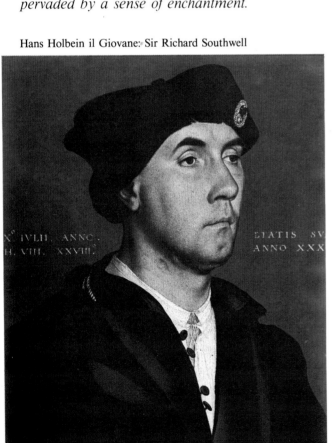

Hans Holbein the Younger

Hans Holbein the Younger was born at Augsburg in 1498 and died in London in 1543; he was one of the most important portraitists of northern Europe in the 16th century. Son of the famous Hans Holbein the Elder, in 1517 he lived in Italy and studied the Renaissance art of Padua. Next he worked in Basel; and when the Protestant Reformation put an end to commissions for devotional works he travelled on to England, where he found a patron in Thomas More. When More lost his position, Holbein was able to find clients among the merchants of the Hanseatic League. He soon gained a considerable reputation and had the chance to work for the court and the aristocracy.
In addition to a self-portrait in pastel the Uffizi has one of Holbein's most famous works, the Portrait of Sir Richard Southwell. *This picture was painted in 1536 and comissioned by some of the most influential members of Henry VIII's court; it displays the great technical skill and refined artistic language of the great German portraitist.*

A. Coreggio: Adorazione

Antonio Correggio

Antonio Allegri (1489-1534) was born in Correggio. It is likely that he acquired his early training in his native town, from his father *and another local artist. Afterwards, he probably went to Mantua where he came under the influence of Mantegna. This hypothesis is supported by a close examination of some of his works: paintings like the* Mystical Mar-

riage of Saint Catherine, *now in the Museum of Detroit, show Correggio's indebtedness to the famous artist from Padua. Other elements of his art – the sfumato, for example, a recurrent technique in Allegri's works – are clearly derived from Leonardo. Correggio, in fact, uses an extremely delicate chiaroscuro to soften planes in painting his figures.*
The most famous of Correggio's works at the Uffizi is undoubtedly the Sojourn in Egypt. *This work was executed for the Church of San Francesco in Correggio and there it remained until 1638 when it was replaced by a copy and the original was transferred to Florence. Remarkable for its extraordinarily balanced composition, this painting strongly reflects the influence of Raphael and Leonardo. The figures of the Virgin and the Child are very delicately modelled, in the style that Raphael adopted for his Madonnas. The softness of the planes is further enhanced by an extremely delicate chiaroscuro, reminiscent of Leonardo's sfumato, and by the light which caresses the objects ceating – as does the still life in the foreground – intensely lyrical effects.*

Andrea Mantegna

Andrea Mantegna was born in 1431 at Carturo, a small island near Padua; he was very lucky in becoming Squarcione's favourite student. Young Mantegna lived and received his training in the beautiful, cultivated Padua, the center of the cultural and artistic ferment of his time. There he came into contact with the creations of a number of Tuscan artists who had worked in the region of Venice – Paolo Uccello, Filippo Lippi, Andrea del Castagno and especially Donatello. The art work they left was a decisive factor in the formation of the Mantegna's style. His art therefore followed the canons of exact perspective and characterization of the figures, which received the sculptural treatment typical of Donatello and the other Florentine artists: but these features were reworked and revivified by the refined code of North Italian Humanism. The classical period, a mythical Golden Age when all things were forged according to a single rule and sole harmony whose measure was man, became the central theme of Manteg-

na's work. These cultivated sources of inspiration were further spurred by the milieu in which Mantegna spent most of his life: the court of the Gonzaga in Mantua. In 1460 the artist had been summoned to this city by the Marquis Ludovic III and there he remained until his death in 1506. Admired and honoured by all, Mantegna left Mantua only on two occasions: in 1466 and in 1467 he journeyed to Florence and from 1488 to 1490 he worked in Rome for Pope Innocent VIII.
His artistic production consists of a large number of frescoes, paintings and graphic works.
The Uffizi houses three of Mantegna's masterpieces: the Portrait of Carlo de' Medici, *the*

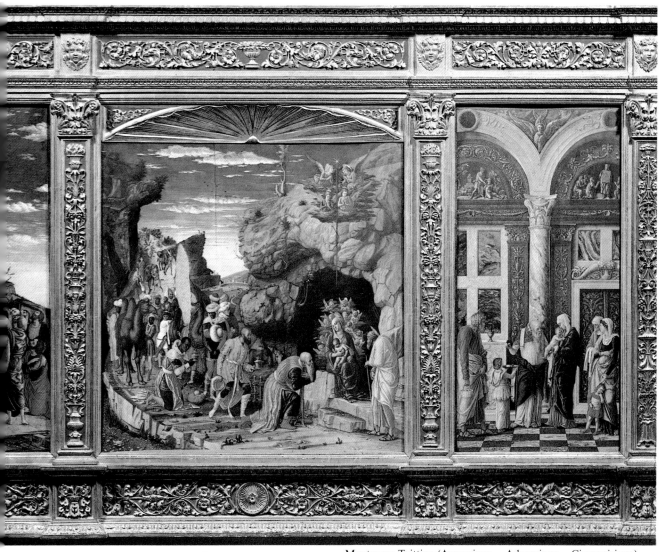

Mantegna: Trittico (Ascensione – Adorazione – Circoncisione)

Madonna delle Cave *and the* Adoration of the Magi. *This last work is a triptych: the panel on the right illustrates the Circumcision, the left the Ascension, and the centre the Adoration of the Magi.*

The adoration centres on a long procession of men and animals which unwinds across a harsh, mountainous landscape until it reaches the grotto of the Child. The biblical episode gives Mantegna the opportunity to create the most diverse human types, all of which are extremely well characterized and meticulously studied in every detail, from their clothes to their headgear. This love of rich detail and the landscape in the background are elements indicating Mantegna's debt to Flemish art. In

the Ascension panel the painter tries to convey the mysticism and intense drama of the event: Christ ascends into heaven, a strong, majestic figure, and solemnly blesses his disciples who, astonished and awestruck, turn their heads towards the Saviour whose last act seems to confirm his promises of salvation and eternal life.

Finally in the last panel the artist shows his unconditional admiration for the classic world, which inspires the postures and clothes of the majestic, lance-armed figures, as well as the setting of the scene, with its luxurious polychrome marbles, its bas-reliefs, its arches and columns, almost a temple from ancient times.

Michelangelo Buonarroti

« I remember how on the sixth day of March, 1475, a son was born to me. I named him Michelangelo; and he was born on a Monday morning four or five hours before the break of dawn; and when he was born, I was the chief magistrate of Caprese, and so he was born in Caprese ».

In this way Lodovico Buonarroti Simoni described the birth of Michelangelo in one of his letters.

The Buonarroti family held a relatively prestigious place in the society of Florence. Moreover, some believed them to be descendants of the Counts of Canossa. For this reason Lodovico was against his son's desire to study painting and drawing. He felt that the career of an artist was contrary to decorum and would disgrace the family name. But Michelangelo's vocation was so strong that nothing could hinder its fulfillment. He was sent to the studio of Domenico Ghirlandaio, an intelligent man who immediately appreciated the boy's enormous talent. After spending a few years in this studio, Michelangelo decided to continue his apprenticeship in the Medici Garden of the Church of San Marco, where Bertoldo di Giovanni taught promising young artists under the patronage of Lorenzo the Magnificent.

The Magnificent's death and the resultant political crisis forced Michelangelo to flee the city, first for Bologna and then for Rome where he set to work on the world-famous Pietà, *finishing it in 1501. Afterwards he returned to Florence and there he worked on a gigantic piece of marble, transforming it into the* David, *for which he was paid the sum of 400 silver coins. During these years he also received a commission to paint the fresco of the* Battle of Cascina *in the Palazzo Vecchio. Michelangelo immediately began working on the cartoon, but in March of 1505 he was forced to interrupt his work, for Pope Julius II had summoned him to Rome. There the artist drew up plans for a gigantic mausoleum for the Pontiff. But a number of misunderstandings caused him to quarrel with the Ecclesiastical Tribunal and he left Rome for his home town. The crisis was resolved after a few months and Michelangelo joined the Pope in Bologna, where he created for the Pontiff a beautiful bronze statue later destroyed during an uprising.*

In 1508 Michelangelo began working on the gargantuan frescoes of the Sistine Chapel, which took him four years to finish.

After the death of Julius II the papal throne was occupied by Leo X, a member of the Medici family, who commissioned Michelangelo to build the Medici-Laurenziana Library, the new Sacristy and facade of the Church of San Lorenzo. For the new Sacristy – which ultimately would become the Medici Pantheon – Michelangelo sculpted four marvelous statues: Dawn, Evening, Day *and* Night. *Giovanni Battista Strozzi the Elder dedicated the following lines to the statue of the* Night:

« Night, that you see sleeping here in graceful pose was sculpted by an angel from the rock. And as she sleeps she lives. If you do not believe me, wake her and she shall speak to you. »

Michelangelo answered him with the following verses:

« 'Tis pleasant to sleep, yet more pleasant it is to be of stone; Since harm and shame are everlasting I find it a blessing to be blind and deaf. So do not wake me. Hush! Speak softly. »

On the 12th of August 1530 the Republic fell: Michelangelo found himself in a difficult situation, but fortunately he was granted a pardon by Clement VII and was able to continue his work on the San Lorenzo Sacristy. Four years later he established himself once again in Rome.

He was well on in years and bothered by numerous ailments, especially kidney troubles, "renella, fianco e pietra", and so Michelangelo stayed in Rome where he had houses and properties; on the 17th of February 1564 death knocked on his door: he was eighty four years old. His nephew Leonardo obtained custody of the body and had it buried with great pomp and solomnity in the Church of Santa Croce in Florence.

The Uffizi has a great work, the Tondo Doni, *the only painting on wood attributed to the master. It dates to 1506 and was painted in honour of the marriage of Agnolo Doni and Maddalena Strozzi. The « Tondo » measures one hundred and twenty centimeters in diameter and cost the buyer one hundred and forty silver coins that were paid after a long and very strange negotiation. According to Vasari: «...When the painting was finished, he sent it to Agnolo's house, covered with a*

Michelangelo: Sacra Famiglia

sheet... and he asked a price of seventy silver coins for it. Agnolo, who was a rather stingy man, thought it strange to spend so much money on a painting, even though he knew it was worth more. He told the messanger that forty coins were enough and gave him that amount. But Michelangelo sent the money back with the message that the price was a hundred coins, otherwise he would take back the painting. Agnolo, who liked the painting, thought: I will give him the seventy silver coins he asked for. But Michelangelo was not content with it: furthermore, incensed at Agnolo's bad faith, he demanded double what he had asked the first time, so that if Agnolo wanted to keep the painting he would have to send him one hundred and forty silver coins».

This work, executed during Michelangelo's youth, represents a landmark in the history of painting. The Holy Family is shown here in an unconventional manner; the style of the painting is clear and precise. The three main characters have been captured in a rotative,

Bachiacca: Cristo a Caifas

twisting movement: this is particularly evident in the figure of Mary. The anatomic details are pictured with great care and show the artist's great familiarity with this element: not in vain did Michelangelo in his youth study anatomy directly from corpses. A group of nudes stands out in the background: these figures are thought to represent humanity and probably have a symbolic meaning. Notice the trick which the artist uses in order to give depth to the painting: the nudes have been deliberately painted out of focus with loosely sketched details, as if the artist's eyes were the lens of a camera. All these innovations make the Tondo Doni an avant-garde work which opened the way to further artistic experiment.

Bachiacca

Francesco d'Ubertino, known as Bachiacca (1494-1557) was born in Florence and worked all of his life in this city. His activity centered on small paintings and the decoration of chests. This minor painter found a source of inspiration in the art of Franciabigio and Andrea del Sarto, but his work was influenced mostly by Durer and Lucas van Leyden.
One of the most interesting paintings by Bachiacca is the Christ before Caiaphas exhibited at the Uffizi. This small panel was inspired by a woodcut of Durer's, in which the German master illustrated the same Biblical subject.

Mariotto Albertinelli

Mariotto Albertinelli (1474-1515) was born and lived in Florence. He was a pupil of Cosimo Rosselli and worked together with Fra Bartolomeo della Porta. He later became a follower of Savonarola and painted exclusively religious works, amongst them the Virgin between Two Saints *(Louvre), the* Annunciation *and the* Madonna and Saints *(Galleria dell'Accademia, Florence).*

The Visitation *is one of Mariotto Albertinelli's finest works. It was executed in 1503 for the Florentine church of Sant'Elisabetta and arrived at the Uffizi in 1786. Notice the feeling for space and the solemn plasticity of the two figures set in the central part of the canvas in front of a typically Quattrocentoesque architectural structure.*

Francesco Granacci

Francesco Granacci (1477-1543) was born and lived in Florence. He was a pupil of Ghirlandaio and a friend of Michelangelo, but in spite of these acquaintances his style evidences the influence of Fra Bartolomeo, whose most important compositions he often imitated.

Amongst Francesco Granacci's most famous works are The Madonna della Cintola *(Galleria dell'Accademia, Florence), the* Saints *(Munich), and* Charles VIII Entering Florence *(Museo Mediceo, Florence).*

M. Albertinelli: La Visitazione

Joseph presents his father and brothers to the Pharaoh *is a large (0.95 x 2.24 m) oil on wood painting; it has been part of the Uffizi collection since 1589. Notice how it shows the painter's interest in detail, how he willingly stops to depict exotic costumes, trees and strange animals.*

Francesco Granacci: Giuseppe presenta al faraone il padre e i fratelli

Raphael

Raffaello Sanzio, known as Raphael, was the only child of the painter from Urbino Giovanni de' Santi and his wife Magia Ciarla. He came into the world on Goog Friday, the 26th of March 1483. Raphael learned the fundamentals of painting from his father who took great care in the boy's education. Noticing Raphael's precocious talent, Giovanni apprenticed him in the workshop of a famous artist: Perugino. Raphael remained at this workshop for eight years and succeeded perfectly in imitating his teacher's artistic vocabulary, as evidenced in his painting of the Marriage of the Virgin *of 1504. In that very same year he broke off his association with Perugino and went to Florence. His experience of the Florentine milieu was a decisive one for young Raphael as it allowed him to study the works of Fra Angelico, Michelangelo and Leonardo at first hand. Until 1508 Raphael alternated between Florence and Perugia; in this period he finished numerous works, including the* Colonna Altarpiece

Raffaello: Madonna del Cardellino (part.)

(Metropolitan Museum, New York), the Ansidei Altarpiece *and the* Dream of the Knight *(National Gallery, London), the* Three Hesperides *(Musée Condé, Chantilly), the* Lady with a Unicorn *(Galleria Borghese, Rome),* The Mute *(Palazzo Ducale, Urbino), the* Madonna del Granduca, *the* Portrait of Agnolo Doni *and the* Portrait of Maddalena Doni *(Palazzo Pitti, Florence).*

In 1508 Raphael moved definitively to Rome where Julius II had commissioned him to decorate the Vatican appartments; there the artist created such masterpieces as the Stanza delle Segnature *and the* Stanza di Eliodoro. *Julius II's successor, Cardinal Giovanni de' Medici, appointed Raphael "Architetto e soprintendente della Fabbrica di San Pietro" with a stipend of three hundred gold coins a year. During Leo's pontificate Raphael executed the frescoes of the* Stanza del Incendio del Borgo, *the tapestry cartoons for the Sistine Chapel, the portraits of* Baldassare Castiglione, Leo X *and* Fedra Inghirami *as well as the* Madonna of the Rocking Chair, *the* Veiled Woman, *the* Fornarina *and the* Transfiguration, *his last work. In fact, Raphael died suddenly on Good Friday, the 5th of april 1520: he was thirty-seven years old.*

In the Uffizi we can admire a number of Raphael's works: for example, his Self-portrait *and the* Portrait of Leo X with the Cardinals Luigi de' Rossi and Giulio de' Medici. *But the most famous work on exhibit at this museum is the* Madonna of the goldfinch. *It measures 1.07 x 0.77 m. and was painted in 1506 for Lorenzo Nasi, a Florentine noble. According to Vasari:* «Raphael had a close friendship with Lorenzo Nasi and as Lorenzo had newly taken a wife he painted him a picture of a child between the knees of the Virgin, to whom a little Saint John is offering a bird to the delight of both. The attitude displays childish sympathy and affection, while the picture is so well coloured and carefully finished that they appear to be actual living flesh. The Madonna possesses an air full of grace and divinity, the plain, the landscape and all the rest of the painting being very beautiful».

In the beginning the Madonna of the goldfinch *had a rather eventful life: on the 12th of November 1547 it remained under the rubble of the Nasi family mansion, which collapsed as the result of a mudslide on the Costa San Giorgio. It was recovered and restored; after-*

Raffaello: Madonna del Cardellino

wards, in 1666, it arrived in the Uffizi.
When Raphael painted the Madonna of the
goldfinch *he was only twenty-three years old;*
but he had already travelled a long way in
his career and had meditated deeply on
Michelangelo's and Leonardo's works. If one
looks attentively at the painting one can see
that the three figures form the pyramidal type

81

of structure so cherished by Michelangelo in his sculptures. On the other hand, the figure of the Virgin and the effects achieved through the use of sfumato clearly reflect the influence of Leonardo. A feeling of peace and serenity extends from the figures over the landscape: nature becomes an integral part of the divine message which always emerges from Raphael's art in an extremely graceful and unaffected manner.

Andrea del Sarto:
Polittico con quattro santi

Raffaello:
Leone X con i cardinali

Andrea del Sarto

Andrea del Sarto, son of Angelo di Francesco, was born in Florence in 1468. He acquired the nickname of «del Sarto» because of his father profession. Once he learned to read and write he was apprenticed to a goldsmith; but a painter named Andrea Barili, who noticed the boy's great talent, took him to his workshop to train him as a painter. Soon afterwards Barili found a master more capable of guiding the boy's extraordinary capacities: Piero di Cosimo «who at the time was held to be among the best Florentine painters» became Andrea's new teacher. After a few years, Andrea broke off with his teacher and opened his own workshop together with Francia, achieving immediate success. During this period the artist finished one on his most famous works: the monochrome frescoes of the Chiostro dello Scalzo, *commissioned by the Compagnia di San Giovanni Battista.*

In 1517 Andrea married a very beautiful woman, Lucrezia di Baccio del Fede, who had been widowed a short time before. It seems that this marriage changed the painter's life for the worse: Lucrezia was a demanding and hard to please wife and Andrea, weak and eaten away by jealousy, was soon completely dominated by her.

The Madonna of the Harpies, *painted in 1517 and now exhibited at the Uffizi, is probably his most famous work. Vasari describes it in the following manner:* «On the right of the Virgin is a fine figure of Saint Francis; his head is expressive of the goodness and simplicity of this holy man. The feet too are very well executed, and so are the draperies, because Andrea arranged the folds softly around the figures in such a way that the outlines of the bodies could be seen. On the right is Saint John the Evangelist as a young man writing the Gospel, in beautiful style. Above the houses is a mist of transparent clouds, and the figures seem to move: this

Andrea del Sarto: Madonna in trono con bambino

painting is held to be one of the most original and beautiful of Andrea's works».

In effect this large tempera on wood (2.07 x 1.78 m) represents one of the culminating moments of Andrea del Sarto's career. The work evinces several stylistic affinities to other maestros: the use of the sfumato technique is clearly indebted to Leonardo while the sculptural treatment of the figure is reminiscent of Michelangelo. The virgin stands statue-like on an ornate pedestal made of stone. The name of the painting originates from the two small harpies represented on the pedestal. Notice the gentle expression on Mary's face who according to some critics in none other than the painters's wife who on this occasion posed as his model.

Pontormo: La cena di Emmaus

Pontormo

Jacopo Carucci, known as Pontormo, was born in 1494 at Pontorme, a village near Empoli. Bartolomeo, his father, was a Florentine painter who had been a pupil of Ghirlandaio: his mother was described by Vasari as « a very virtuous and good young woman ». *Jacopo's childhood and adolescence were marked by an impressive series of mournings. Within a few years he lost his father, his mother, his grandparents and a sister. Misfortune and poverty deeply influenced his personality, which Vasari described as introverted and neurotic. Except for two trips to Rome, Pontormo spent all of his life in Florence; and*

there he lived completely isolated from the rest of the world. Tradition has it that his misanthropy led him to live in a room on a high storey which could be reached only by climbing a rope ladder that the artist immediately pulled back with a special pulley.

This psychological portrait certainly comes close to the truth for it has been confirmed by Jacopo's own diary, which displays a neurotic personality, full of fears and maniacal thoughts.

In spite of his "difficult" personality Pontormo succeeded in making a name for himself in his profession. Protected by the Medici, respected and highly thought of by the men of his time, he soon became known as a man of genius, open to the new artistic experiences that were being introduced in Italy. In fact, Pontormo's art has a stylistic affinity not only with such Italian painters as Michelangelo, but also with the art of Durer, whose works he had had the opportunity to see. These two influences combine to create his Mannerism, tense and dramatic, ambiguous and provocative, with its beautiful, unreal colours reminiscent of Caravaggio's or El Greco's palette.

This "avant-garde" painting reached its climax in the frescoes at the choir of San Lorenzo of which no trace remains and which left the contemporary public rather puzzled.

The Uffizi houses several works by Pontormo, including the Portrait of Cosimo the Elder, founder of the Medici dynasty, who died in 1464.

Another one of Pontormo's famous works preserved at the Uffizi is the Supper at Emmaus, painted in 1525 for the Certosa del Galluzzo. Many critics have seen in this work a number of elements that anticipate the art of the 17th century and especially that of Caravaggio. Let us examine the realistic elements that Pontormo introduced into this magnificent composition: the faces of the Apostles, the humble meal on the table, the domestic animals peeping out from under it. It seems almost as if the painter had tried to infuse life into a classical subject of religious art, to take in all he could of the everyday by portraying the faces and expressions of the people who walked the streets of his city. But these commonplace, real characters are placed in an atmosphere of mystical tension and supernatural feeling a feature which further accentuates the artistic complexity of Pontormo, leader of the Tuscan Mannerist school.

Vasari

Bachiacca: storie di S. Acacio

Bronzino: Sacra Famiglia

Agnolo Bronzino

Angiolo di Cosimo di Mariano Todi, known as Bronzino, was born in 1503 at Monticelli, a small village near Florence. His family was very poor. Bronzino was apprenticed to Pontormo who felt for him an almost fatherly affection. He worked almost exclusively in Florence where in the beginning of his career he had attained a reputation for his works at the Certosa, Santa Felicita, la Badia and Santa Trinita. In 1530 he left Florence for Pesaro where the Duke of Urbino, Guidobaldo, had commissioned from him the decoration of the Villa Imperiale. Two years later he returned to Florence and helped Pontormo to paint the frescoes in the Medici Villa at Poggio a Caiano. In 1539 he was one of the artists who prepared the scenery and decorations for the wedding of Cosimo and Eleonora

da Toledo. As a result of this great occasion the painter established close ties with the ducal house and was appointed court painter; during this period he also began his activity as a portraitist. In fact, in 1540 he portrayed the noble Bartolomeo Panciatichi and his wife Lucrezia in two masterpieces of invaluable beauty which reveal all his mastery. These portraits were followed by those of the Medici family members, amongst them the Portrait of the Grand Duke Cosimo I, *(1545), the* Portrait of Giovanni dei Medici *(1545), the* Portrait of Pia, natural daughter of Cosimo I *(1542).*

After he became a famous artist Bronzino continued working to a great extent for the grand duke's family, which commissioned him to do work upon work. He died in 1572 at the age of sixty nine, loved and respected by all his contemporaries. During his lifetime he had cultivated a sincere friendship for Vasari, who in his « Lives » praises Bronzino not only as an artist but also as a man: « ...Bronzino was a very gentle and well-mannered friend; his conversation was pleasant, and he was very honest in his affairs. He was as generous and kind with his things as a noble artist can be. His nature was peaceful, and he never did wrong unto anyone, and he always loved the courageous men who were his colleagues, as I know, for I have had a close friendship with him for forty three years, that is from 1524 until this year ».

In the Uffizi we will find many paintings by Bronzino, amongst them a number of portraits of Medici family members. The most famous of these is the Portrait of Eleonora da Toledo and her son Giovanni, *probably because it was chosen as the image which symbolized the Medici Exhibition of 1980.*

The picture was painted between 1544 and 1545 and portrays Eleonora, the daughter of the Spanish viceroy of Napoli who married Cosimo in 1540, and her son Giovanni. The duchess wears a rich brocade wedding dress, finished in pearls and precious stones, the same dress she was buried in, as confirmed by an inspection of her tomb in 1857. This oil on wood is a clear example of Bronzino's cultured and refined courtly Mannerism: the purity of the serene, detached faces, the solemn bearing of the figures and the richness of detail all contribute to create a splendid image, the exaltation of an ideal of regal dignity.

Tiziano Vecellio: Eleonora della Rovere

Titian

Tiziano Vecellio, known as Titian, was born in 1490 at Pieve di Cadore. His family was «one of the noblest of those parts» *and* «at the age of ten he showed great intelligence and a good temper and was sent to an uncle, an honorable citizen of Venice, who perceived his bent for painting and apprenticed him to Gian Bellino, an excellent and very famous painter». *About 1507 Titian broke off with his Master and went into Giorgione's workshop. The following year we find him still working in Venice on frescoes at the Fondaco dei Tedeschi.*

Tiziano: La Flora

Tiziano Vecellio: Venere del cagnolino

TIZIANO

Tiziano Vecellio: Venere d'Urbino

The Uffizi exhibits several paintings by Titian, the most famous of which are the Flora and the Venus of Urbino.
Flora *(0.79 x) arrived at the Uffizi in 1793. It was painted by Titian in 1520-22 and portrays a beautiful young woman who some critics believe to be Violante, Palma the Elder's daughter, with whom the painter had fallen in love. The young woman is shown from the knees up in a slightly informal pose: her blouse flutters from her shoulder, baring part of the breast. The image is drawn with thick and continuous brushstrokes, for in this period of his career Titian's style reflects the influence of the Venetian school which relies on colour to model and create form. The only indication of depth in the painting derives from a gesture made by the young woman, who seems to want to show us her roses; and it is to this gesture that she owes her name of "Flora".*
Even more famous is the Venus of Urbino, *painted in 1538 for Guidobaldo della Rovere, Duke of Urbino. Vasari had the opportunity to see the painting in Urbino and describes it in the following manner:* «...The same Duke's wardrobe contains two graceful female heads by Titian and a young recumbent Venus surrounded by flowers and delicate draperies of great beauty».
According to some art historians the painting portrays one of the Duke's favourites, for apart from her beauty she possesses no other attributes that might qualify her as a goddess from Olympus. The painting remained in Urbino until it was sent to Florence as part of Vittoria della Rovere's dowry; and in 1776 it was placed in the Uffizi.

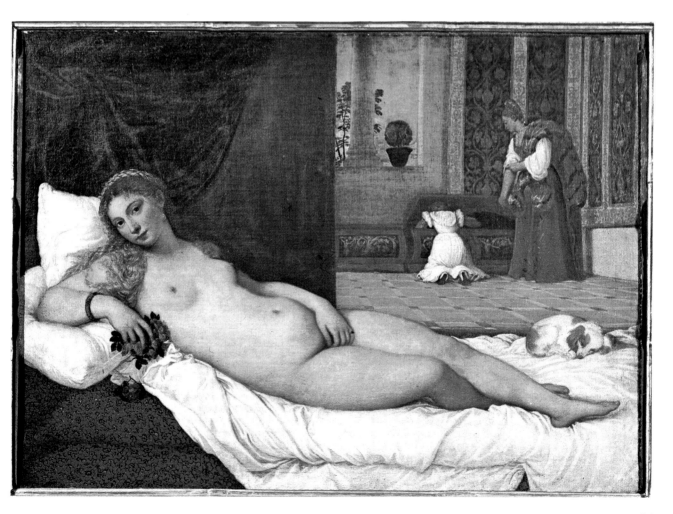

Jacopo Palma il Vecchio: Sacra Famiglia

Palma the Elder

Jacopo Negretti, known as Palma the Elder was born in 1480 at Serina, a small village near Bergamo, and died in Venice in 1528. He is generally considered to be one of the greatest Venetian artists. Inspired by Vivarini, Bellini and Giorgione, Palma developed a style of his own, characterized by well-defined figures set against luminous and serene landscapes.

Amongst his most famous works there stand Venus and Cupid *(Cambridge),* Three Sisters *(Dresden),* Portrait of a Poet *(London),* Madonna and Child between two Saints *(Church of Santo Stefano, Vicenza) and the tryptych of* Saint Barbara, Saint Dominic and Saint Sebastian *(Church of Santa Maria Formosa, Venice).*

The Uffizi Gallery exhibits three works by Palma the Elder: The Resurrection of Lazarus, the Holy Family with Saint John and Mary Magdalene *and* Judith. *This latter work is undoubtedly the most famous one of the three. It was painted shortly before the artist's death and is an example of his serene and luminous art. Judith is not portrayed as a strong-willed, merciless woman after the execution of her terrible deed, but appears as a Venetian noblewoman, elegant and serene, who with great indifference holds up the sword and bloody head.*

Parmigianino

Francesco Mazzola, known as Parmigianino, was born in Parma in 1503. The uncles who raised him were two obscure painters who nevertheless recognized the boy's great talent and encouraged it. Francesco was a bad-tempered and churly boy, but he was also a child prodigy. He began painting at a very young age and imitated the style of Correggio who at the time was working in Parma. About 1523 he received his first important commission: he was to decorate the private rooms of Paola Gonzaga, wife of Galeazzo Sanvitale, in the fortress of Fontanellato. These frescoes are strongly indebted to Cor-

Parmigianino: Madonna dal collo lungo

L. Mazzolino: Strage degli Innocenti

reggio's paintings in the Camera of San Paolo, *yet they also present some novel Mannerist elements which probably derive from the work of Anselmi, a painter whom Parmigianino had met in Parma.*

Once the work commissioned by Paola Gonzaga was finished, Parmigianino went to Rome. Although he was not very successful, his roman period was very important for his artistic development for there he had the opportunity to see the works of Michelangelo and Raphael at first hand. Also, in Rome he participated in the meetings held at the house of Paolo Valdambrini, secretary to the Pontiff, where he met Pierin del Vaga, Giulio Romano and Rosso Fiorentino and where he was able to probe deeper into the Mannerist theories. In 1527 the sack of Rome took place and Francesco went to Bologna, where he stayed for four years, until 1521. In the Emilian capital Parmigianino applied all he had learned during his stay in Rome. Two of his works from this period, the Saint Rocco *of* San Petronio *and the* Madonna *of Santa Margherita, show an increasingly complex, more intellectual vocabulary, in spite of some lingering Correggian elements. Afterwards the artist returned to Parma and there he was commissioned to paint a series of frescoes at the church of Santa Maria della Steccata. Parmigianino was rather dilatory in completing this work, for he was not particularly*

interested in it and was in no great hurry to finish it. After a few years he had concluded only a small part of the frescoes; and so his clients had him arrested and imprisoned.

The Uffizi houses Parmigianino's most famous painting: the Madonna and Child with Angels, *also known as the* Madonna of the long neck. *This oil on wood (2.19 x 1.35 m) is a late work of the artist and was painted for the Chiesa dei Servi in Parma. The painting shows a truly unusual image of Mary: her body is elongated and supple, her perfectly oval face is supported on an extraordinarily long neck, her flesh seems to be made of wax. The bearing of the figure and the clothes show the artist's technical virtuosity in handling form. The Child is lying on Mary's lap; his elongated figure and waxy flesh colouring are disturbing, but most of all it is the total abandon of his body that shocks the observer. On Mary's right we see a group of children, the angels, portrayed as elegant figures with sinuous bodies and sweet, but somewhat ambiguous expressions. It is obvious that all these figures have a symbolic value, which is further enhanced by the metaphysical landscape in the background and the small figure of the prophet at Mary's feet. All these elements tend to increase the fascination that this mysterious and disturbing masterpiece exerts on the observer.*

Garofalo

Benvenuto Tisi (1481-1559) was a Ferrarese painter whose works were influenced first by Giorgione and later by Titian. In 1515 he went to Rome and there he came into contact with Raphael's art. It evidently made a great impression on him, for his late paintings clearly evidence the influence of the Master from Urbino.

The Annunciation by Garofalo exhibited at the Uffizi is a mannered painting that presents with great elegance and mastery of execution the typical elements related to the subject.

Garofalo: Il Cristo della moneta

Dosso Dossi

Giovanni Luteri, known as Dosso Dossi, was born in 1489 and became one of the most important Ferrarese painters. He received his training in Venice and there he met many famous artists. Shortly thereafter he entered into the service of Duke Alfonso d'Este and remained with him all his life. Dossi died in Ferrara in 1542. He was a very talented painter: his skilled use of colour and the turbulent style of his works foreshadowed the art of the 17th century.

Two of Dosso Dossi's most important works are The Departure of the Argonauts *(National Gallery, Washington) and the* Virgin with Saint George and Saint Michael *(Este Gal-*

lery, Modena).

The Uffizi collection includes several paintings by Dossi, one of which – Witchcraft *– is a particularly interesting one. The meaning of this work is highly mysterious, so much so that the title is continually debated, and sometimes it is known as the* Bambochade *or the* Allegory of Hercules.

In it the artist has portrayed a crowd made up of the most disparate figures: a faun, two women and several well-characterized male figures. The women's attitude is typically classic: the profile of one seems to have been taken directly from a cameo. Notice the sculptural treatment of the figures and the painstakig delicacy with which the artist describes the objects in the foreground, reminiscent of a 17th century still life.

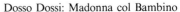

Dosso Dossi: Madonna col Bambino

Sebastiano del Piombo

Sebastiano Luciani, known as Sebastiano del Piombo, was born in Venice in 1485. After learning the fundamentals of painting at Giovanni Bellini's workshop he became one of Giorgione's assistants and probably worked with him on the frescoes at the Fondaco dei Tedeschi. In 1517 he went to Rome, where he studied the paintings of Raphael and worked at the Villa Farnese and at the Church of San Pietro in Montorio. In 1526 he returned to Venice; but the Eternal City continued to fascinate him and three years later he settled down definitively in Rome. He became a friend of Michelangelo's and was deeply in-fluenced by him, although their friendship ended abruptly in 1534. Thirteen years later, in 1547, Sebastiano del Piombo died in his adoptive city.

Amongst the painter's most important works are the frescoes of The Metamorphosis *at the Villa Farnese,* Dorotea *(Staatliche Museen, Berlin) and* Cardinal Carondelet with his secretary *(Thyssen Collection, Lugano).*

The Uffizi houses several of Sebastiano del Piombo's works, including the Death of Adonis. *This large canvas illustrates the famous myth of Venus and Adonis. Notice the gentle, melancholy lacustrine landscape inspired by Giorgione's compositions, and the sculpturesque nudes clearly derived from Michelangelo.*

Sebastiano del Piombo: La morte di Adone

Lorenzo Lotto

Lorenzo Lotto was born in Venice in 1480. He carried out most of his activity in Bergamo and in the Marches. His youthful style in deeply indebted to the works of Bellini, Giorgione, Antonello da Messina and Durer; only in one of his early paintings, the Portrait of the Bishop Bernardo de' Rossi (now in the Galleria Nazionale di Capodimonte), the influence of the Venetian masters gives way to a more personal style. This potrait is markedly true to life; the artist shows an abundance of details and several naturalistic traits, elements that are probably a result of Lotto's contacts with northern European art. On the other hand, the colours and the approach to chromatic harmony are still typically Venetian, derived from painters like Bellini and the young Titian. To the artist's youthful period belong the Sacra Conversazione *(Galleria Borghese, Rome), the* Saint Christina Altarpiece *now in Treviso and the* Saint Dominic Polyptych *at the Pinacoteca Civica of Recanati, a city where the artist had worked in 1508. The altarpiece, the culminating point of Lotto's youthful experience, is still closely related to the Venetian painting of the 15th century. Lotto succeeded in going beyond this phase as a result of a trip to Rome, where he had the opportunity to work with Raphael. The Umbrian master did not remain indifferent to his assistant's art; on the other hand, the paintings Lotto executed after his Roman period reflect the influence of Raphael. Amongst these works are the* Deposition *(Pinacoteca Civica, Jesi) and the* Altarpiece with St. Bartholomew and St. Bernard, *a painting in which the artist's mature style has achieved its full expression. In 1524, after a*

Lorenzo Lotto: Sacra Famiglia

short and unfortunate journey to Venice, we find Lotto once again in Bergamo. In this northern Italian city he completed the decoration of the Suardi Chapel *at Trescore, a true masterpiece for the compositional freshness of the scenes with St. Barbara and St. Clare. This feeling for a simple, lively narrative style also characterizes the* Stories of the Virgin *at San Michele near Bergamo and the marquetry work of the choir of Santa Maria Maggiore, executed after one of Lotto's drawings.*

After his Bergamesque period the artist moved to the Marches where he produced several masterpieces, including the Annunciation *(Pinacoteca di Jesi) a work in which he represents the evangelical subject in a truly innovative way.*

The Uffizi possesses a beautiful painting by Lotto: the Holy Family. *This work was signed and dated in 1534 and belongs to the artist's mature production. Despite the elements obviously derived from Venetian painting, the style of the work is completely personal: notice the feeling of intimacy, a typical feature of Lotto's compositions, from the* Annunciation *of Jesi to the frescoes of St. Barbara and St. Clare. Always in line with the intimate, domestic mood of his work, this picture presents a remarkable innovation for Italian art: the Virgin is portrayed as a young woman, held between the knes of Saint Anne.*

G. Pagani: Susanna al bagno

Jacopo Chimenti:
Il sacrificio di Isacco

Jacopo Zucchi: L'età del Ferro

Empoli

Jacopo Chimenti (Florence 1551-1640), known as Empoli, was a member of a group of artists which tried to introduce innovations into Florentine painting of the late 16th century. In spite of some «Classical» tendencies, his style is characterized by the naturalistic tones typical of 17th century art.

The Drunken Noah exhibited at the Uffizi is a very interesting painting. It was done in oil on a copper plate at about the end of the 16th century. The trees, the vineleaves and the figure of Noah in an attitude of abandonment, are portrayed with a realism already imbued with the style of the 17th century.

A. Bronzino: Pietà

François Clouet

François Clouet was born in Tours in 1510 and died in Paris in 1572. His father Jean was a renowned artist and François also attained a considerable reputation; on his father's death, he succeeded him as painter of the court.

In the Uffizi we can admire the Portrait of Francis I King of France *by Clouet. This small painting contains all the elements of the art of Clouet, who was one of the most important exponents of the French Mannerist school.*

Paolo Veronese: Ester condotta da Assuero

Paolo Veronese

Paolo Caliari, known as Veronese, was born in 1528 in Verona. He was apprenticed at the workshop of a minor painter from his city named Badile and was influenced by the works of Giulio Romano, Correggio and Parmigianino. In 1523, after working at San Fermo and Castelfranco, Veronese went to Venice where he remained until his death. There he began to work at the Church of San Sebastiano, and very soon became a succesful and renowned artist. In 1560, he went to Rome with the Ambassador of Venice and had the opportunity to see Michelangelo's and Raphael's masterpiece at first hand.

Amongst his most famous works are the Portrait of the Cuccina Family, *now in Dresden, the* Wedding at Cana *(Louvre) and several version of the* Last Supper. *This last subject was one of the artist's favourites, for it allowed him to construct group pictures containing sumptuous backgrounds filled with architectonic structures. His imagination and his love for decorative pomp were the cause of a trial which almost had serious consequences. It all started when the Dominican friars of SS. Giovanni e Paolo commissioned him to do a painting of the* Last Supper *(now at the Accademia), to replace another work on the subject by Titian, previously destroyed during a fire. Veronese started to work with his usual*

Paolo Veronese: Sacra Famiglia

enthusiasm and when the painting was finished he presented it to the friars. But his clients were scandalized by the profanity and opulence of the canvas: in fact, the composition is filled with an incredible array of richly clothed figures as well as dogs, dwarves and jesters. Veronese was summoned to the tribunal of the Inquisition and tried. When he was called to make his deposition, he defended himself by stating that it had not been his intention to create a blasphemous picture and concluded by saying that «...we painters take the same liberties as poets and madmen take». This incident didn't have serious consequences and Paolo was able to continue his fortunate career without any problem. In 1575 he started to paint the Venice and Virtue *allegories and five years later he conclud-ed the* Love Allegories, *now at the London National Gallery. One of his last works was the portrait of* Lucrezia, *in which the sharp tones evidence a sensibility already close to the Baroque. Veronese died in Venice in 1588, at the age of sixty.*
The Uffizi houses several of Veronese's works, including the Holy Family with St. Barbara and St. John. *This canvas, a great master-piece, was painted in the early 1560s. The whole of Veronese's world is shown in the composition: elegance, refinement and har-mony all emerge in the sweet family scene centered around the Child. The refined and elegant figures of Mary and the Saints have been given sculptural treatment. And notice the fashionable clothes and Saint Barbara's magnificent head of hair!*

Tintoretto: La Samaritana

Tintoretto

Jacopo Robusti was born in Venice in 1518. His father was a silk dyer and it was this profession that earned young Jacopo the nickname of Tintoretto, by which he is universally known. According to tradition Tintoretto was a pupil of Titian, but it is more likely that he developed his style under the influence of the formal elements of Mannerism introduced in Venice by artists like Sansovino, Pordenone, Sebastiano del Piombo and Vasari.

Tintoretto started working in Venice about 1540 and in 1564, after having painted a number of frescoes for the Scuola Grande di San Marco, he was commissioned to decorate the Scuola Grande di San Rocco. He devoted the following twenty years of his life to this job, decorating the halls and the hotel with his magnificent work. At the same time he carried out several other assignments, assisted by three of the eight children he had fathered by his wife Faustina Episcopi. Marco, Domenico and Marietta learned their father's profession working with him on the numerous private and public commissions he received. By then he was famous. In the Palazzo Ducale Tintoretto painted several canvases, including one, the Paradise, *which measures 200 square*

Tintoretto: Leda

Tintoretto: Cristo al pozzo

metres and is the largest painting in the world. In his last period he continued to execute majestic compositions with the overcrowded scenes that he had always liked. That is how such masterpieces as the Battle of Zara came to see the light. The Last Supper, painted at the end of his life, was commissioned by the Church of San Giorgio Maggiore, and he worked on it until his death in his native city in 1594.

Tintoretto is one of the most important Venetian painters. Many saw in him the genius who could blend Titian's colouring and Michelangelo's design.

F. Barocci:
La Madonna del Popolo

Federico Barocci

Federico Fiori, known as Barrocci, was born in Urbino in 1535. In 1555 he travelled to Rome for the first time and there he studied the art of the masters of the early 16th century. In 1561 he returned to Rome a second time to fresco the villa of Pius IV.

He continued to work in Urbino and Perugia, and died in his home town in 1612. Barocci, like many other painters of his time, was inspired by the artists of the preceding generations. He studied the works of Raphael, Lotto and Titian, though Correggio was the artist he admired most.
The Uffizi exhibits several works by Barrocci,

P.P. Rubens: Ritratto di Filippo IV

P.P. Rubens: Isabella Brandt

including the Madonna del Popolo. *This large painting was executed between 1576 and 1579 for the Confraternita della Misericordia of Arezzo. It portrays the blessing Christ and Mary who dominate a happy and surprised crowd of people. Notice how painstakingly Barocci has described the physiognomical traits and sweet expressions of the smiling children in the foreground.*

Pieter Paul Rubens

Pieter Paul Rubens was born at Siegen, Westphalia, in 1577. In 1600, after finishing his training in the Belgian city of Antwerp, Rubens travelled to Italy for the first time. He stayed for a while in Venice and there he had the opportunity to see the works of Veronese, Titian and Tintoretto at first hand. Shortly afterwards Vicenzo Gonzaga, Duke of Mantua, enlisted him in his service and Rubens followed his new patron to Florence for the Marriage of Maria de' Medici and Henry IV of France. He remained in the duke's service for eight years, during which period he had the opportunity to visit several Italian cities, including Genova and Rome, and Florence once more in 1603. These trips allowed him to acquire a deep knowledge of Italian art, especially of the masterpieces painted by Raphael and Michelangelo. In 1608 he returned to Antwerp where a year later he married Isabella Brant. In the meantime his reputation had increased: Rubens's workshop became renowned and artists like Van Dyck and Jan Brugel could be found working there. Rubens worked unceasingly to fulfil the demands of illustrious clients: Maria de' Medici commissioned from him two enormous pictorial cycles, one on her life and the other on her husband Henry IV. The great Flemish painter died in Antwerp in 1640 at the age of seventy three.
Ruben's art ushers in a new chapter in the history of art: the Barroque.

P.P. Rubens: Tra il Vizio e la Virtù

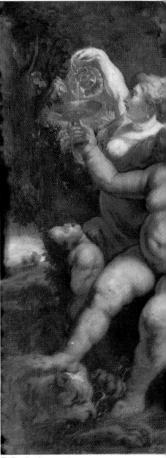
P.P. Rubens: Baccanale

Justus Sustermans

Justus Sustermans was born at Antwerp in 1597. In his early youth he began to cultivate painting and attained a certain success with a series of celebratory works. Later he settled in Florence where he was appointed official portraitist to the Medici court. He died in the Tuscan capital at the age of eighty-four. Amongst his most famous works are the portraits of Christina of Denmark *and* Charles of Lorraine, *now exhibited at the Pitti Palace in Florence.*
The Uffizi houses one of his most renowned works: the Portrait of Galileo Galilei. *This work was commissioned from the painter by the scientist himself who later gave it as a present to his friend Elia Diodati. The canvas is characterized by an intense, warm light that bathes the face of the great scientist and sets the details in relief.*

J. Sustermans: Galileo Galilei

Anthony Van Dyck

Sir Anthony van Dick was born in Antwerp in 1641 and started his artistic career at the age of sixteen. Shortly thereafter he journeyed to England and in 1621 he visited a number of Italian cities, including Genoa, Rome,

Antoine Van Dyck: Carlo V

Florence, Bologna and Palermo. In 1630 he returned to Antwerp and two years later he settled down definitively in London, where he died in 1641.

Van Dick was one of the most sought-after Flemish painters of the 17th century and his works served as an example for portraitists of later years.

Vaso mediceo

Sala della Niobe

A
1 COPIA ROM. DA ORIG. GRECO –   FANCIULLO
2 COPIA ROM. DA ORIG. GRECO –   FIGLIO DI NIOBE
3 COPIA ROM. DA ORIG. GRECO –   FIGLIO DI NIOBE
4 COPIA ROM. DA ORIG. GRECO –   FIGLIO MINORE DI NIOBE
5 COPIA ROM. DA ORIG. GRECO –   FIGLIA MAGGIORE DI NIOBE
6 COPIA ROM. DA ORIG. GRECO –   NIOBE E FIGLIA MINORE
7 COPIA ROM. DA ORIG. GRECO –   SELENE (LUNA)
8 COPIA ROM. DA ORIG. GRECO –   VASO MEDICEO
9 COPIA ROM. DA ORIG. GRECO –   FIGLIA DI NIOBE
10 COPIA ROM. DA ORIG. GRECO –   FIGLIO DI NIOBE
11 COPIA ROM. DA ORIG. GRECO –   FIGLIO DI NIOBE
13 COPIA ROM. DA ORIG. GRECO –   FIGLIA DI NIOBE
14 COPIA ROM. DA ORIG. GRECO –   IL PEDAGOGO
15 COPIA ROM. DA ORIG. GRECO –   FIGLIO MAGGIORE DI NIOBE
17 COPIA ROM. DA ORIG. GRECO –   MUSA
18 COPIA ROM. DA ORIG. GRECO –   FIGLIO DI NIOBE
19 COPIA ROM. DA ORIG. GRECO –   PSICHE TORMENTATA
20 COPIA ROM. DA ORIG. GRECO –   FANCIULLO
21 COPIA ROM. DA ORIG. GRECO –   CAVALLO

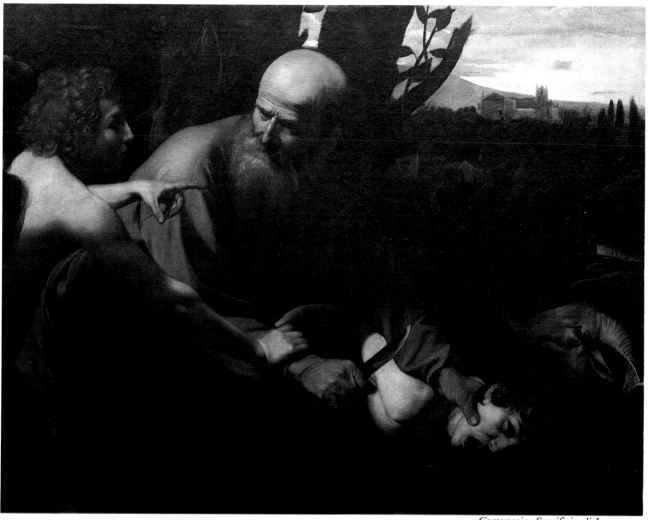

Caravaggio: Sacrificio di Isacco

Caravaggio

Michelangelo Merisi was born in 1573 in Caravaggio, a small town from which he took his artistic name. In 1584, at the age of eleven, he went to Milan; there he worked in the studio of Simone Peterzano, a Mannerist painter from Bergamo. In 1588 he finished his apprenticeship and went to Rome. The first few years in this city were extremely hard for young Caravaggio, who had already shown «some extravagant tastes resulting from his great ardour and spirit». *In Rome he worked as an assistant to Cavaliere d'Arpino and Grammatica; Pandolfo Pucci and Cardinal del Monte were his patrons. After finishing his apprenticeship he established himself as an independent master and soon his great painting skill became evident. In his early works, Caravaggio dealt with genre subjects such as* the Tricksters, The Gypsy fortuneteller, Young Boy with a fruit basket,

Boy bitten by a lizard *and, to a lesser extent, with religious subjects like* Mary Magdalene, *and* the Rest on the Flight in Egypt. *Mythology also provided a source of inspiration for the young painter. It led him to create a number of works, including* Sick Bacchus, Bacchus, *and* Victorious Love. *Although these were recurrent subjects in the painting of the time, Caravaggio's treatment of them was new as far as content and pictorial expression were concerned. The* Bacchus, *now at the Uffizi, is represented as a young village boy; his head is crowned with vines and he is wearing a classic-style toga. The young God holds a cup of wine in his hand, in a convivial gesture, while in the foreground there is a bottle and a basket of fruit. The painter obviously refers to the mythological subject, but the painting lacks the idealized form which until then had prevailed in that tradition. Caravaggio has represented the pagan God as a young man and he purposely hints at a*

Caravaggio: Medusa

number of objects common to everyday life, without translating them into an idealized language. Therefore the god of wine is dressed in a simple sheet and he reclines not on a triclinium but on an ordinary bed. The great innovations in Caravaggio's works raised a great deal of controversy, for many thought that the young painter wanted to desecrate tradition. This accusation was especially violent in ecclesiastical circles which at the time were the main buyers of religious art and whose members were particularly powerful in Rome.

In May 1606 the painter's life was upset by a very serious event. Caravaggio, who was well-known for his impetuous and violent nature, frequently became involved in unpleasant situations, but his influential patrons had always managed to get him out of trouble. On May 29th 1606 the painter took part in a game of pallacorda (an old version of the game of tennis) with a man called Tomma-

sini. During the game a quarrel broke out and soon it degenerated into a fight. Tommasini struck Caravaggio first, but he was mortally wounded in return. No one could save Caravaggio from the charge of murder. The painter found refuge with the Colonna family and afterwards fled to Naples. The Madonna del Rosario, the David (now in Vienna) and the Seven Works of Mercy in the church of Pio Monte della Misericordia belong to this period and are all works of great significance for the development of Neapolitan painting of the seventeenth century. Caravaggio abandoned the light tones of his early Roman works: his colours became darker, and the main figures were illuminated by beams of light from above.

Caravaggio's forced stay in Naples did not last very long. The artist left for Malta in 1608. On the island his paintings became even gloomier and more dramatic, as is evident in Saint Jerome, the Beheading of John the Baptist (both in the cathedral of La Valletta) and the Sleeping Cupid at the Pitti Palace. The painter's troubled painting reflected the drama of his life, just as it was about to come to a tragic end. Less than a year after his arrival on the island he offended the very powerful Order of the Knights of Malta, which resolved to kill him and set a number of paid assassins on his trail. The painter fled for safety, which became more and more difficult to find. He sought refuge in a number of cities: Syracuse, Messina, Palermo, and finally he sailed for Naples, arriving there in the autumn of 1609. In the city of Naples the assassins of the Order of Malta recognized him and attacked him. He was seriously injured and left for dead. Before he had fully recovered from his injuries the artist decided to return to Rome for he had received the news that the Pope had granted him a pardon. He travelled by sea to Porto Ercole and there was arrested by mistake. Two days later he was released but, in the meantime, the boat had vanished and all his belongings with it. This was a tremendous shock for the unfortunate Caravaggio who, overcome by despair, started wandering aimlessly on the beach where he died under the hot summer sun on the 18th of July 1610.

The Uffizi houses some of Michelangelo Merisi's most important works. Since we have already spoken about the Bacchus let's turn now to another famous painting: The Head

Caravaggio: Bacco

of Medusa. *This oil on canvas was originally set on a wooden disc: it was commissioned from the painter by Francesco Maria del Monte, who wished to present it to Francesco I de' Medici, the Lord of Tuscany at that time. The Grand Duke had it placed on the arm of a suit of Oriental armour that had been given to him by the Shah of Iran. Although there are some doubts about its date of execution, art historians have placed it between the final years of the sixteenth century and the beginning of the seventeenth. In fact, the face of the Medusa, resembles that of both the cleric and the scoundrel in the* Martyrdom of Saint Matthew *(1599-1600); therefore it is possible that the* Head of the Medusa *was painted at the same time. With this gift, Francesco Maria del Monte probably wished to pay homage to the Prince, for the head of the mythological monster had a profound allegorical meaning in the Renaissance.*

Guercino

Giovanni Francesco Barbieri, known as Guercino, was born at Cento in 1591 and died in Bologna in 1666. In the beginning of his artistic career he was inspired by the works of Scarsellino and Dossi. In his maturity he travelled to the north of Italy and to Rome and as a result of these trips his art absorbed some elements derived from the painting of northern Europe.
Amongst his most important works we can mention Saint William of Aquitaine Receiving the Habit *(Pinacoteca, Bologna),* Et in Arcadia Ego *(Galleria Corsini, Rome).*
The Concert Champêtre *exhibited at the Uffizi is a small oil on copper plate executed about 1617. It is one of the painter's early works: notice, in fact, how the landscape and the figures have been inspired by the art of Dosso Dossi.*

Guercino: Diporti estivi

Claude Lorrain

*Claude Lorrain was born at Nancy in 1600
but he moved to Rome in his early youth. He
spent all his life in the Eternal City and died
there in 1682. Lorraine's oeuvre consists
mostly of landscapes and mythological scenes.
His paintings attained great success and his
style was imitated by many painters of his
time. In order to combat forgery, Lorrain
wrote a* Liber Veritatis, *a catalogue now
found at the British Museum in London,
where he listed the buyers and dates of execution of his works.*
Amongst his most famous paintings are The
View of a port at dawn *(Louvre),* Landscape
with the nymph Egeria *(Galleria di Capodimonte, Naples) and* Mercury stealing Apollo's oxen *(Galleria Doria Pamphili, Rome).*
*The Uffizi Houses one of Lorraine's most
famous works:* A Port with the Medici Villa.
*This canvas was commissioned from the
painter by the Cardinal Carlo de' Medici and
painted about 1637. Notice how painstakingly
the artist has represented the details, from the
boat shrouds to the faces of the common
people, from the architectural elements to the
objects of everyday life. Notice also his mastery in the use of light, light that falls sharply
from the sun and alights gently on the sea,
on the faces of the figures and on the objects
strewn across the beach.*

Claude Lorrain: Porto con Villa Medici.

Rembrandt: Ritratto di vecchio

Rembrandt

Harmenszoon Van Rijn, better known as Rembrandt, was born at Leiden in 1606. His father was a well-to-do miller; and the easy economic circumstances of his family allowed Rembrandt to dedicate himself to his studies. In 1620 he registered at the University of Leiden, but soon after he followed his natural inclination for art. He learned the fundamentals of painting at the workshop of Jacob Van Swanenburgh and completed his studies in the studio of Peter Lastman. A few years later he opened his own studio in Leiden and, once he had attained a certain success, he left his home town and settled in Amsterdam. In the great port of the Netherlands Rembrandt worked frantically and soon the increase in his reputation brought him considerable profits. Within a few years be won great fame and was sought after by the Flemish bourgeoisie who commissioned from him a great number of portraits. In 1634 he married Saskia, who brought him a rather important sum of money as her dowry. Rich, famous and honoured by all, Rembrandt bought a sumptuous house in the Jewish district, and filled it with an inmense collection of valuable art objects. His life passed happily for a good many years, and then suddenly luck turned her back on him. In fact, he lost his wife and three of his children within only a few years;

Civetta: Miniere di rame

Rembrandt: Autoritratto giovanile

his commissions diminished noticeably and his uncontrolled spending got him more and more into debt. Finally his economic situation collapsed: in 1656 he was declared bankrupt and all his belongings, including his art collection, were auctioned off. Rembrandt retired to a small room which he shared with his second wife and his surviving children. His success had gone forever and he spent the last years of his life a humble and lonely man, until his death in 1669. Rembrandt's oeuvre is enormous; in fact, the Dutch artist had continued to paint until the end of his days. His paintings are distributed throughout the most important museums of the world although, obviously, the largest part of his work in concentrated in the Netherlands. The Uffizi has on exhibit several of Rembrandt's portraits, including his Self-portrait as a young man *which was probably painted about 1634. The artist from Leiden was a very versatile painter, capable of attempting a wide variety of subjects; and in this he differs from his Dutch colleagues who generally specialized in only one genre. The portrait was a youthful passion of Rembrandt's to which he owed, among other things, a large part of his earnings.*

This painting demonstrates how Rembrandt's portraiture strongly differs from that of his contemporaries. The painter doesn't just give us a pompous or realistic image of himself; rather, he penetrates his very own soul, studying its most hidden elements only in order to represent them later in the face. In this way he suceeds in creating a strong psychological painting, which analyzes the subject's personality and achieves effects of great beauty and force. These signs of modernity are quite evident in Rembrandt's Self portrait as a young man, *in which the skilled use of colour and the flood of light on the face indicate the artist's strong will and his self assurance in facing life.*

Rachel Ruysch

Rachel Ruysch was born in Amsterdam in 1664. Her father was the famous Frederic

Rachel Ruysch: Frutta e insetti

A. Watteau: Il flautista

Ruysch, the greatest anatomist of the 16th century, the scientist, mentioned by Giacomo Leopardi, who had invented a liquid in which corpses, animals, plants and flowers could be preserved. His laboratory was considered to be a veritable land of marvels and even the Czar of Russia, Peter the Great, paid it a visit. Rachel, the daughter, became a distinguished artist and inherited her father's passion for the precise, scientific description of animals, flowers and fruit. She specialized in still life painting and gained considerable fame in Europe. Her works are few, since her minute exploration of detail required a very long time to carry out. Rachel Ruysch died in Amsterdam in 1750 at the age of eighty six.
Among Rachel Ruysch's most famous works are Study of Flowers *at the National Gallery in London,* Vases of Flowers *at the Hague Museum and* Large Vase of Flowers *at the Museum of Ghent.*
At the Uffizi is the panel by Rachel Ruysch called Fruit and Insects. *This beautiful, perfectly pictured still life was executed in 1711 for the Grand Duke Cosimo III de' Medici, a passionate collector of still life works.*

117

Jacob Van Ruisdael

Jacob Van Ruisdael was born in Haarlem in 1628. He first studied painting with his father Isaak, then with his uncle Salomon. A precocious, talented boy, he soon excelled his masters and within a very short space of time became a famous painter. Van Ruisdael's main subject was the landscape, which he painted with great emotional power and formal perfection. He wished to show the majestry and power of nature in his work. For this reason he loved to portray storms and ancient forests. Jacob Van Ruisdael died in Amsterdam in 1682. His opus consists of nearly fifty paintings.

Among Van Ruisdael's most famous works are The Jewish Cemetery, now in Dresden, The Tempest, at the Louvre, View of Haarlem in Berlin and The Windmill at Wijk in Amsterdam.

The Uffizi exhibits one canvas by Jacob Van Ruisdael, the Landscape with Shepherds and Farmers. It is a late work and shows a typical Dutch country landscape.

Canaletto: Canal Grande – Venezia

Jacob Van Ruysdael: Paesaggio

Canaletto: Palazzo Ducale – Venezia

Canaletto

Giovanni Antonio Canal, known as Canaletto, was born in Venice in 1697. His father was a theatrical scene painter and in the beginning of his career Canaletto followed this profession. At the age of twenty he abandoned theatrical painting and began to dedicate himself only to his art. It is likely that the first subjects depicted by Canaletto were fantastic landscapes with ruins, a very popular genre at the time. Afterwards he started working dir-

ectly from nature and from 1730 on he achieved marvellous results. Most of his landscapes were views of Venice and its surroundings. He painted canals, palaces, gondolas and boats in full daylight, highlighting every detail, from the gondoliers' clothes to the most minute architectural elements. For these views the artist often used a «camera ottica», a device by which a lens throws onto a ground glass screen the image of a view, in order to better define the perspectival structure of the vast foreshortened panoramas he portrayed. The results were remarkable and the artist

Francesco Guardi: Arco e marina

Pietro Longhi: La Confession·

Francesco Guardi: Arco e pontile

soon gained a considerable reputation. His work was highly esteemed and famous not only in Venice but in other European countries as well, and most of all in Great Britain. The Uffizi houses two classic canvases by Canaletto: View of the Canal Grande and View of the Palazzo Ducale. The latter work is one of the most famous of the artist's «vistas», in fact there are numerous copies of it, all of them signed by Canaletto. The views of the Canal Grande can be divided into two types: those with the Bucintoro, the magnificent boat used by the Doge's ambassadors, and the others, like the one in the Uffizi,

which portray the lagoon filled with boats and gondolas. Notice how carefully the artist depicts the details, using light to define them to perfection. The view is animated by the dynamism of the figures, each caught in a completely natural pose. Notice, for example, the dignified bearing of the passangers sitting in the gondolas, and the efforts of the rowing boatmen, bent over their oars. Canaletto thus became the great portraitist of the 18th century Venice which, after centuries of power and glory, was slowly undergoing a melancholy but splendid decline.

J. M. Nattier: Maria Zeffirina di Francia

G.B. Tiepolo: Statua di un imperatore

Pietro Longhi

Pietro Falca, nicknamed Longhi, was born in Venice in 1702. He studied painting in the workshop of Balestra and this led him to begin producing mainly religious or heroic and mythological works. Later he devoted himself exclusively to the portrayal of everyday scenes set in his native city. It was in this role, as a realistic genre painter, that Longhi acquired considerable fame. He died in Venice in 1785.

Among Longhi's most famous works are the Dance Lesson *and* Concert *at the Galleria dell'Accademia of Venice, the* Concert *at the Brera Gallery in Milan, the* Swoon *and* Blind Man's Buff *at the National Gallery in Washington, the* Presentation *at the Louvre and the* Dentist *at the Galleria dell'Accademia in Venice.*

There is one canvas by Longhi at the Uffizi: the Confession. *This painting is a perfect example of the work of Longhi, who combined a sharply observant mind with a spirit of subtle irony in describing the society of Venice of his time.*

Jean Marc Nattier

Jean Marc Nattier (1685 - 1766), a highly successful painter, was born and worked in Paris. He was employed by the court of Louis XV, who esteemed his elegant, luminous painting. Nattier portrayed the aristocrats of the French court in the guise of mythological characters. He represented Marie Adelaide as Diana *and* Madame Henrietta as Flora.

G. M. Crespi: La Pulce

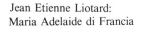

Giuseppe Maria Crespi

Giuseppe Maria Crespi, known as Lo Spagnolo, was born in Bologna in 1665. He became famous as a painter quite early, and was protected and aided by the Grand Duke Ferdinand II de' Medici, who purchased many of his works.
Among Crespi's most famous works are the Cottage *and the* Library of Music *in Bologna. Several works by Crespi are exhibited at the Uffizi. Among them is the* Flea, *a small oil on copper representing a folk scene, a fairly successful genre at the time.*

Jean Etienne Liotard:
Maria Adelaide di Francia

Jean Etienne Liotard

Jean Etienne Liotard was born in Geneva in 1702. He first studied painting in Geneva and later in Paris. He eventually returned to Geneva, where he died in 1789.
Liotard was a typical 18th century figure, He sought out new experiences, tried a variety of

techniques in his painting and undertook long
voyages through Europe and Asia. His works
was centered on landscapes and a variety of
images of everyday life.
Among Liotard's major works are Madame
d'Epinay and Portrait of a Woman in Turkish Dress at Geneva, and Girl Selling Cho-
colate at Dresden.

The Uffizi collection contains one work by
Liotard, the Portrait of a Woman, known as
Marie Adelaide of France in Turkish Dress.
It is a lovely canvas showing the French noblewoman immersed in reading. Notice how
the painter lingered over every fine detail of
the girl's exotic costume.

Giovan Battista Piazzetta

Giovan Battista Piazzetta was born in Venice in 1683. The son of the sculptor, he turned to painting at an early age and was influenced mainly by Crispi. When, later, he opened a studio in Venice, it because famous in no time at all. In 1750, when Piazzetta was one of the most highly esteemed artists of his time, he opened a school. This school later became the Accademia. Piazzetta died in 1754.

Piazzetta's most famous works are Saint James Martyr, *at the Church of San Stae, the* Glory of Saint Dominic, *at San Zanipolo, the* Assumption, *at the Louvre, and the* Fortune-Teller, *at the Galleria dell'Accademia in Venice.*

The canvas by Piazzetta at the Uffizi is Susanna and the Elders. *This painting, executed about 1720, is interesting for its narrative approach to the famous episode as well as for its use of light, which models the features, faces and bodies of the characters.*

J. B. S. Chardin:

J. B. S. Chardin:

Jean Baptiste Siméon Chardin

Jean Baptiste Siméon Chardin (1699 - 1779) was one of the major French painters of the 18th century. He was under the protection of Louis XV and highly thought of throughout Europe for his ability to reveal the poetry of the most humble objects and most common everyday scenes in his art.

Among Chardin's major works are the Copper Fountain, Boy with a Top, Still life with a Pipe *and* Self Portrait, *all at the Louvre.*

Chardin often reproduced his most successful works. Copies of this kind are the two canvases at the Uffizi: Girl with a Shuttlecock *and* Youth with a House of Cards.

Corridoio Vasariano (da via della Ninna)

The Vasari corridor

It is impossible to complete a description of the Uffizi without mentioning the Vasari Corridor, built by Cosimo I in 1565 when his son Francesco married the archduchess Joanna of Austria. The long elevated Corridor connects the Uffizi to the Palazzo Pitti, first passing over the Ponte Vecchio and then continuing along Via Guicciardini. From the windows of the Vasari Corridor one can enjoy extremely evocative views; from an opening, the work of, Buontalenti one can see the interior of the Church of Santa Felicità and from another window the visitor can admire the beautiful and harmonious Boboli gardens.

Gli Uffizi (lato sud)

Ponte Vecchio e Corridoio Vasariano

Ponte Vecchio   Torre Mannelli

Index of the Artists

Editors' Note: The numbers in heavvy print refer to the illustrations

EDITRICE S.D.F.   Via Pandolfini, 39r Firenze - Tel. 055/211515   • *Translation:* Geoffrey Rowland •

Direttore responsabile: Maurizio Mannelli • *Redazione:* Daniela Moriani • *Grafica:* Amalia D'Angela • *Testi a cura di:* Luigi Pruneti • *Fotocomposizione:* Fotolito Tassinari • *Montaggi:* Elleti • *Stampa:* Grafiche Alinari e Baglioni • *Documentazione fotografica:* Archivio fotografico della Casa Editrice • Copyright Aprile 1987 • Riproduzione anche parziale vietata • *Distribuzione:* A-Z Souvenir, via Ghibellina, 174r. - Firenze - Tel. 055/214821